John R. Pescosolido
Professor Emeritus
Central Connecticut State University
New Britain, Connecticut

Reviewers

Anita Uphaus
Coordinator of Early Childhood Programs
Austin Independent School District
Austin, Texas

Deanna Dove
Education Specialist for Grades K–1
Orange County Public Schools
Orlando, Florida

Patricia D'Amore
Assistant Literacy Coordinator
Cooperative Educational Services
Trumbull, Connecticut

Dr. Donna Ronzone
Principal and Director of Special Education
Briggs Elementary School District
Santa Paula, California

STECK-VAUGHN
ELEMENTARY • SECONDARY • ADULT • LIBRARY
A Harcourt Company

www.steck-vaughn.com

Acknowledgments

Editorial Director Stephanie Muller
Senior Editor Amanda Sperry
Assistant Editor Julie M. Smith
Associate Director of Design Cynthia Ellis
Senior Design Manager Cynthia Hannon
Designer Deborah Diver
Media Researcher Sarah Fraser
Editorial Development, Design, and Production The Quarasan Group, Inc.
Cover Illustration Rose Berlin
Senior Technical Advisor Alan Klemp

PHOTO CREDITS

9 ©Park Street/SV; 12 (rat) ©Robin Redfern/Animals Animals; 14 (wag) ©Alfred B. Thomas/Animals Animals; (well) ©Amy C. Etra/PhotoEdit, Inc.; (win) ©AFP/Corbis; 16 (jog) ©Bruno Maso/Photo Researchers, Inc.; 18 (nap) ©Superstock, Inc.; 20 (hit) ©Bill Aron/PhotoEdit, Inc.; (rat) ©Robin Redfern/Animals Animals; 22 (rat) ©Robin Redfern/Animals Animals; 25 (zoo) ©John M. Roberts/Corbis Stock Market; 37 (well) ©Amy C. Etra/PhotoEdit, Inc.; (keg) ©John Olson/Corbis Stock Market; 38 (well) ©Amy C. Etra/PhotoEdit, Inc.; 38 (fell) ©Park Street/SV; 41-42 (hit) ©Bill Aron/PhotoEdit, Inc.; 43 (dot) ©Park Street Photography; 43, 45 (ox) ©Fulvio Roiter/Corbis; 45 (spot) ©Johnny Hernandez/Stone; 46 (dot) ©Park Street Photography; 50 (hug) ©Myrleen Ferguson, PhotoEdit, Inc.; 55 (ran) ©Michael Newman/PhotoEdit, Inc.; 61 (bookmobile) ©Elena Rooraid/PhotoEdit, Inc.; 79 (big) ©David Fleetham/FPG International; 93 ©Margot Conte/Animals Animals; 97 ©Stephen Simpson/FPG International; 105 ©Superstock, Inc.; 107 (play) ©Rick Patrick/SV; 109 ©Ariel Skelley/Corbis Stock Market; 121 ©Mary Kate Denny/PhotoEdit, Inc.; 139, 142 (zoo) ©John M. Roberts/Corbis Stock Market; 141 ©The Zoological Society of San Diego. Additional Photography by: Comstock Klips, Corbis, Eyewire, Inc., PhotoDisc, Inc., Steck-Vaughn Collection, and Stockbyte.

ART CREDITS

Robert Alley 81, 99; Sheila Bailey 120; Shirley Beckes 76, 116, 147; Mircea Catusanu 65, 108, 124, 140; Randy Chewning 84, 104; Shelley Dieterichs 123, 125; Karen Dugan 72, 85, 92; Julie Durrell 57, 75; Cynthia Fisher 80, 101, 129, 144; Ruth Flanigan 128, 136; Dara Goldman 64, 112, 149; Mike Gordon 77; Benrei Huang 68; John Kanzler 89, 102; Anthony Lewis 137, 150; Erin Mauterer 96, 132; Yoshi Miyake 36 (vet), (jet), (men), 40 (fox), (fin), (lip), 44 (fox), 48 (pup); Dan Sharp (fox mascot); Sherry Neidigh 117, 126; Cary Pillo 56, 78, 88, 100; Janet Skiles 113, 133; Dorothy Stott 60.

ISBN 0-7398-3609-9

Printed in the United States of America
10 11 12 WC 08 07

The words *duck, fox, road,* and *tree* are hidden on the cover. Can you find them?

Contents

Unit 5

Unit 6

Study Steps to Learn a Word

1. **Say** the word.
   What sounds do you hear?

2. **Look** at the letters in the word.
   Think about how each sound is spelled.
   Close your eyes.
   Picture the word in your mind.

3. **Spell** the word aloud.

4. **Write** the word.
   Say each letter as you write it.

5. **Check** the spelling.
   If you did not spell the word correctly,
   use the study steps again.

Use the steps on this page to study words that are hard for you.

Spelling Strategies

What can you do when you aren't sure how to spell a word?

Say the word aloud. Make sure you say it correctly. Listen to the sounds in the word. Think about letters for the sounds.

Guess the spelling of the word and check it in a dictionary.

Write the word in different ways. Choose the spelling that looks correct.

rad rid red

Draw the shape of the word to help you remember its spelling.

cold

Choose a rhyming helper and use it. A rhyming helper is a word that rhymes with the word and is spelled like it.

cat—mat

Create a memory clue to help you remember the spelling.

The tree is by the street.

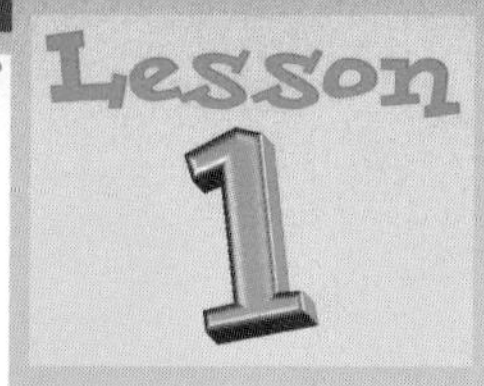

m, d, f, g

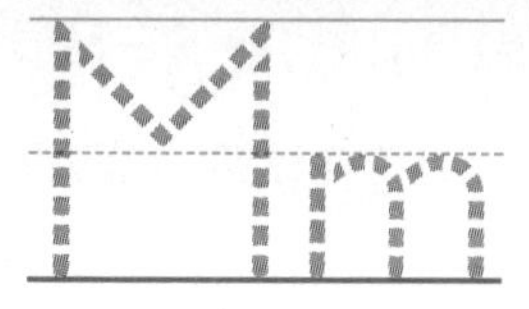

mop

Mop begins with the m sound.
Write m if the picture name begins with the m sound.

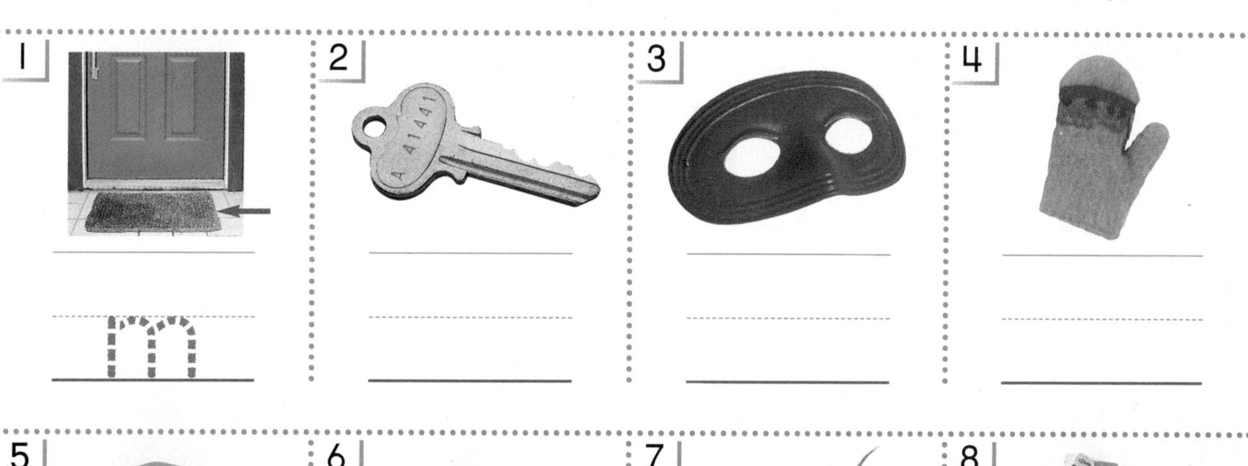

Ham ends with the m sound. Write m if the picture name ends with the m sound.

ham

Dog begins with the d sound. Write d if the picture name begins with the d sound.

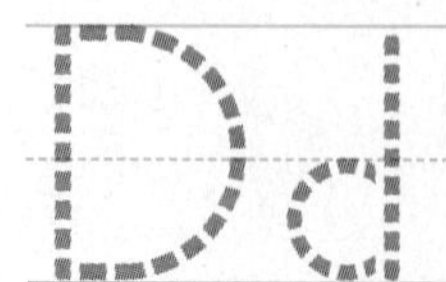

dog

1 dad

2 uck

3 ig

4 oll

5 esk

6 oor

7 ig

8 un

Bed ends with the d sound. Write d if the picture name ends with the d sound.

bed

9 li

10 sa

11 ca

12 roa

Name ______________________________

Fan begins with the f sound. Write f if the picture name begins with the f sound.

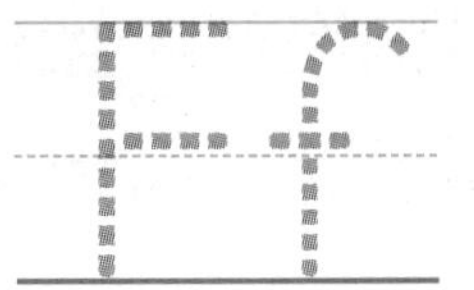

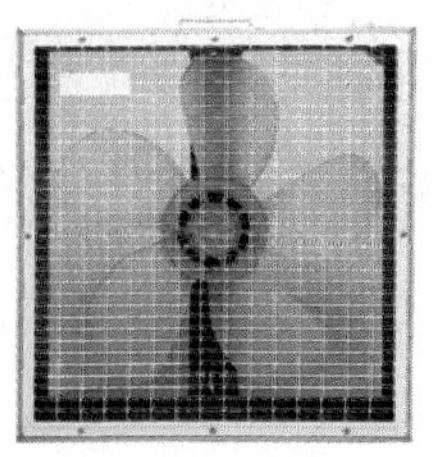

fan

1

2

3

4

5

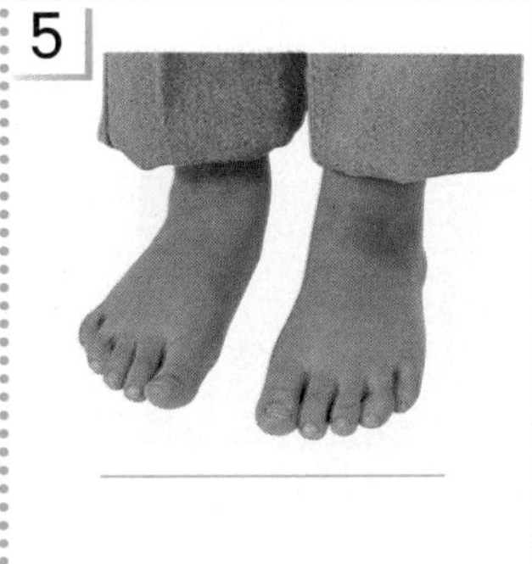

6

7

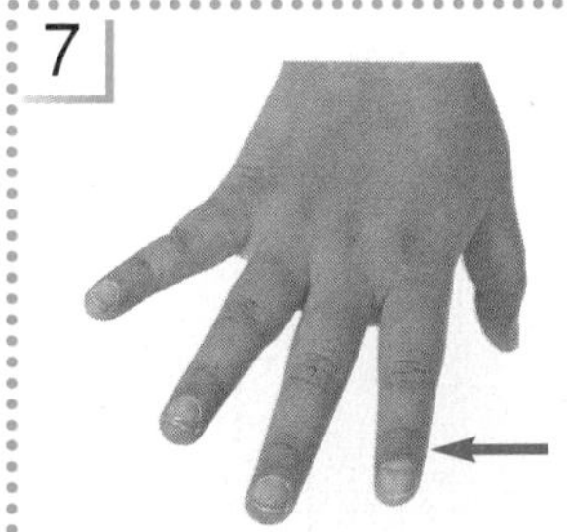

8

Leaf ends with the f sound. Write f if the picture name ends with the f sound.

leaf

9

10

11

12

Gum begins with the g sound.
Write g if the picture name
begins with the g sound.

Gg

gum

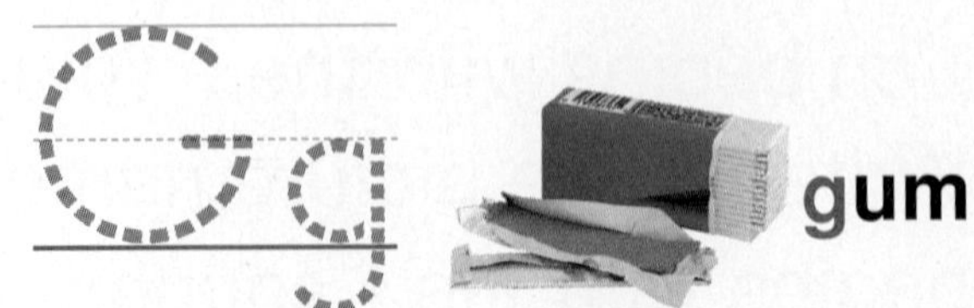

1

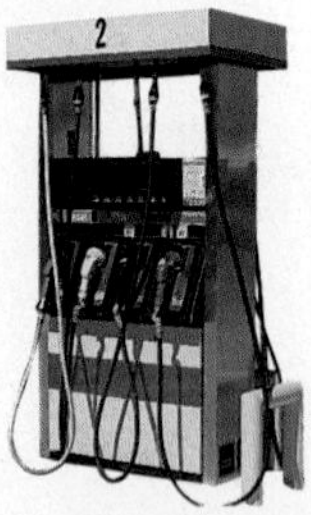

gas

2

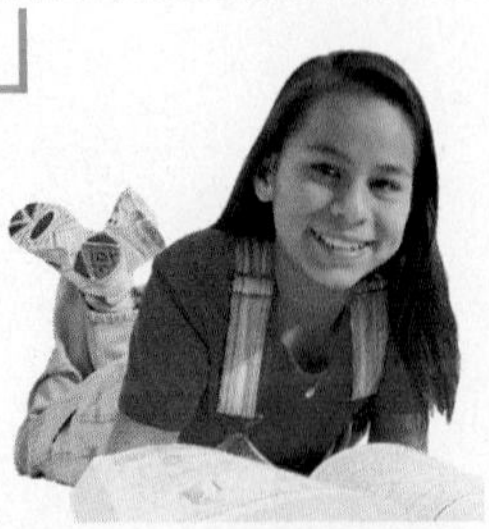

irl

3

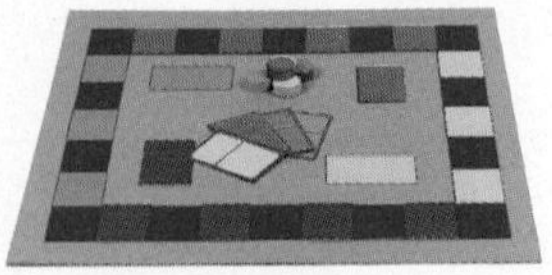

ame

4

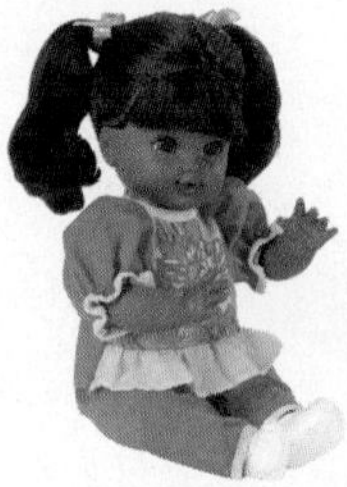

oll

5

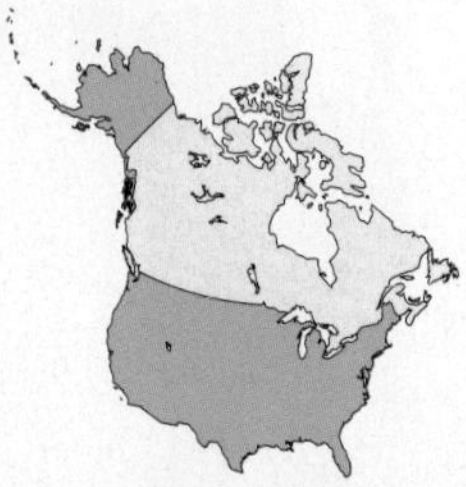

ap

6

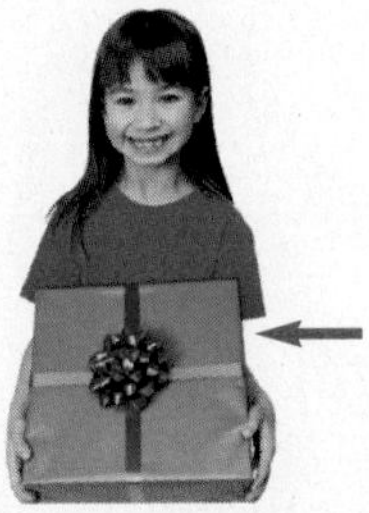

ift

7

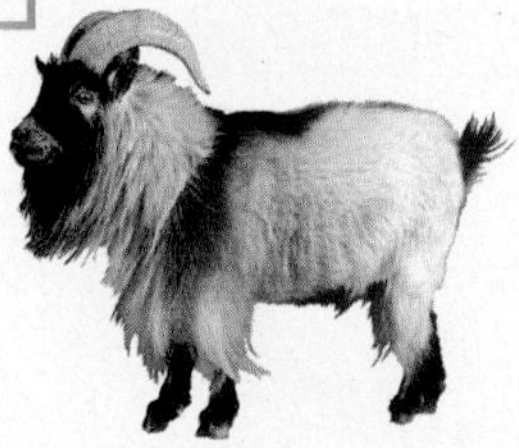

oat

8

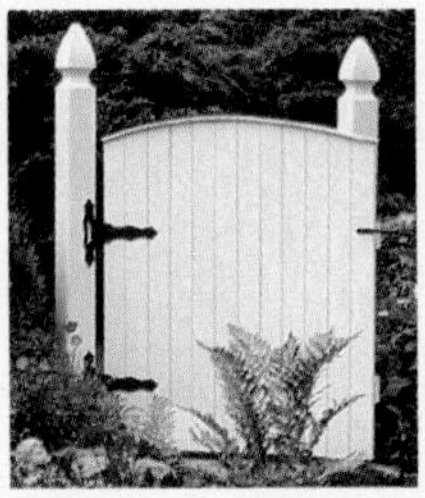

ate

Log ends with the g sound. Write g if the
picture name ends with the g sound.

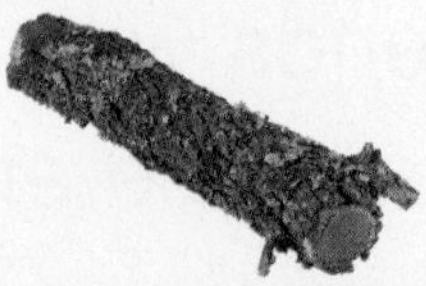

log

9

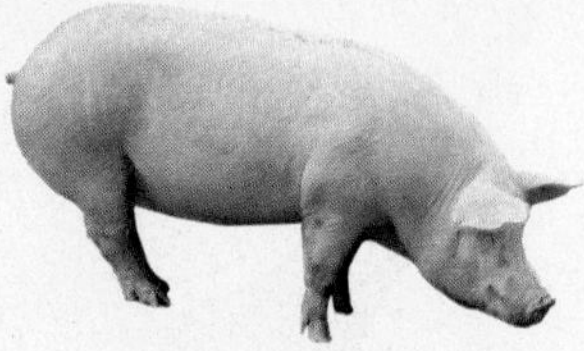

pi

10

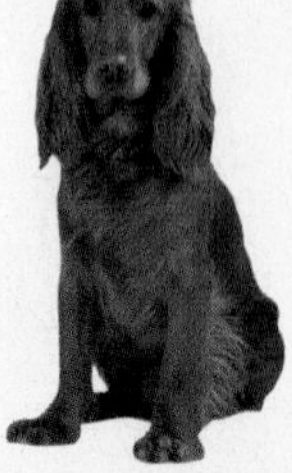

do

11

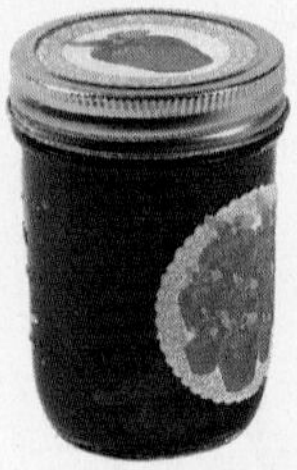

ja

12

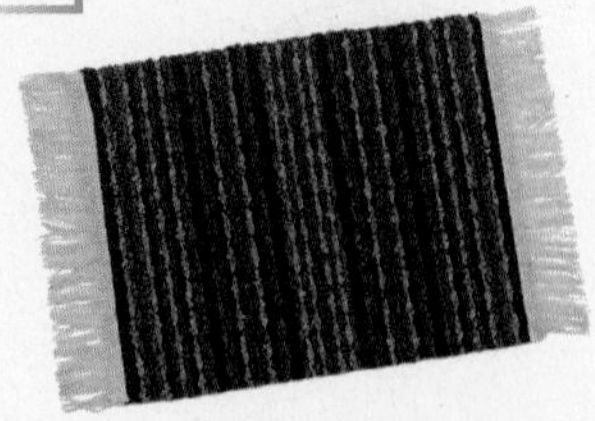

ru

Name ______________________________

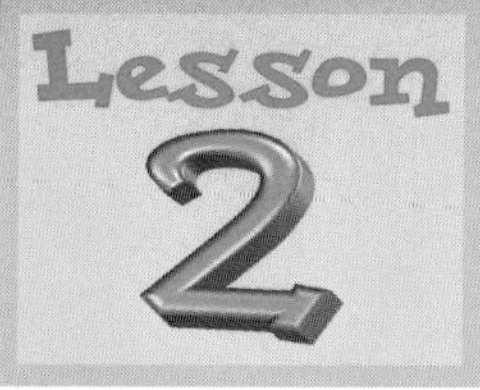

b, t, s, w

Bb

bell

Bell begins with the b sound.
Write b if the picture name begins with the b sound.

Tub ends with the b sound. Write b if the picture name ends with the b sound.

tub

9 

10 

11 

12 

Ten begins with the t sound.
Write t if the picture name
begins with the t sound.

Tt

ten

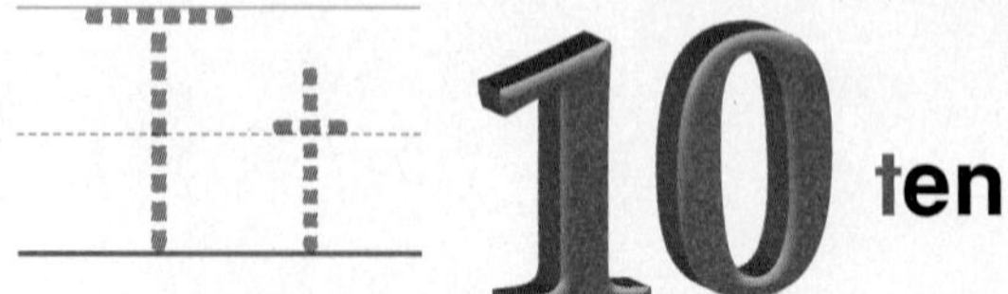

1 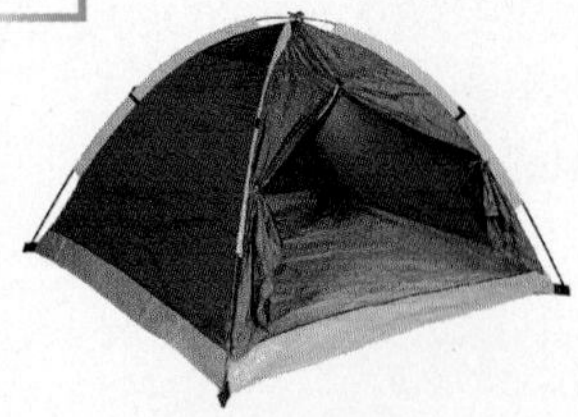

tent

2 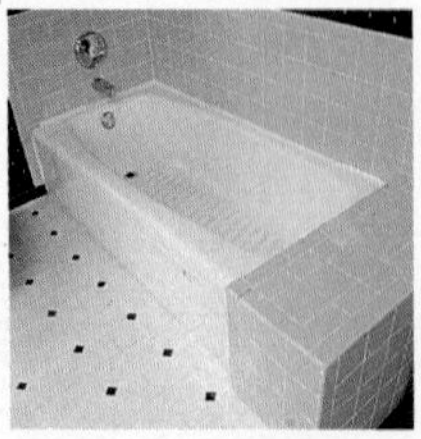

ub

3 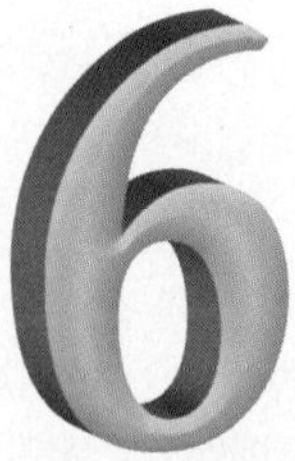

ix

4 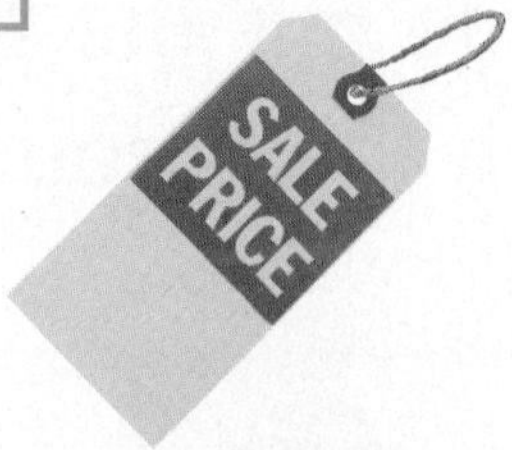

ag

5 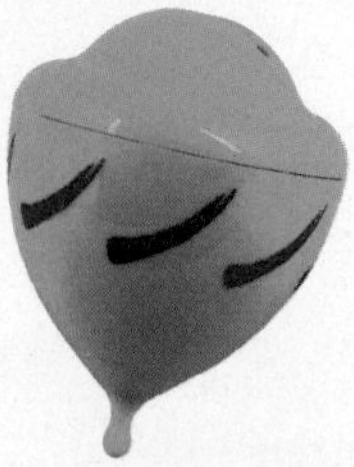

op

6 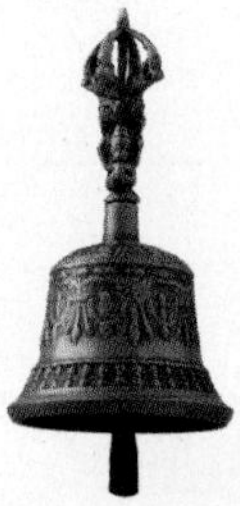

ell

7 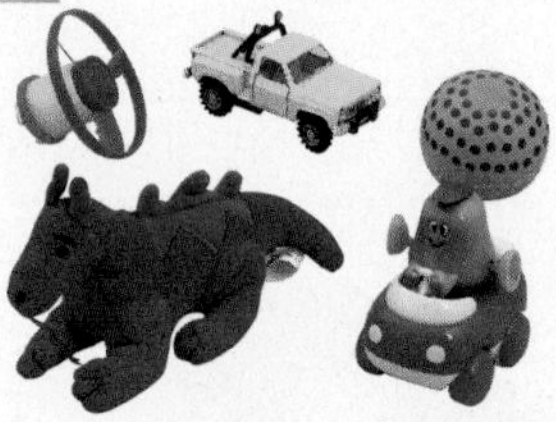

oys

8 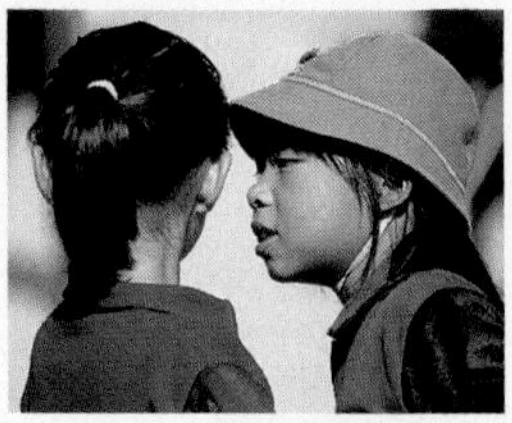

ell

Net ends with the t sound. Write t if the
picture name ends with the t sound.

net

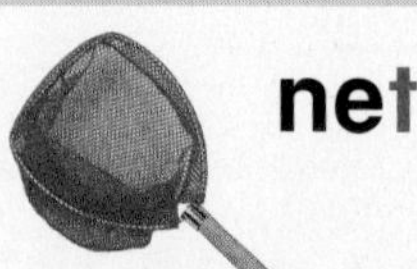

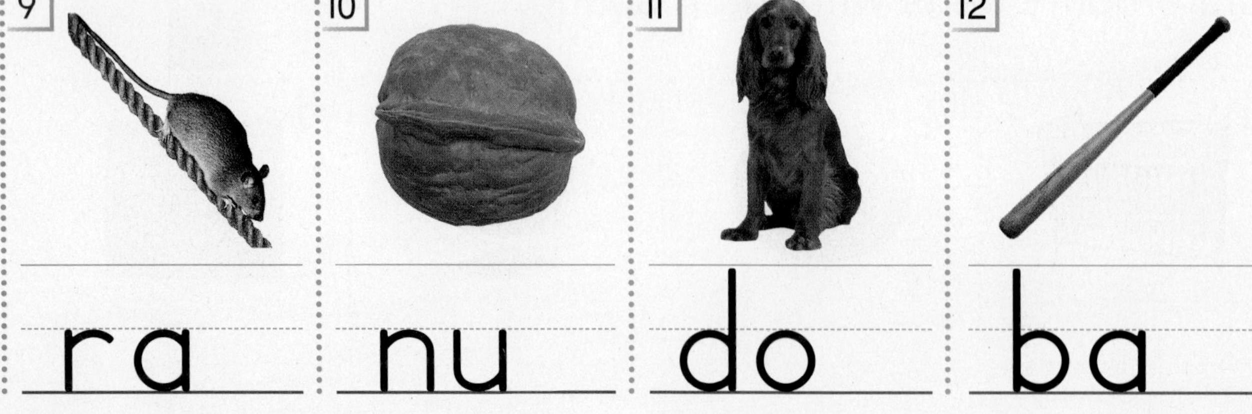

9

ra

10

nu

11

do

12

ba

Name ____________________

Sun begins with the s sound. Write s if the picture name begins with the s sound.

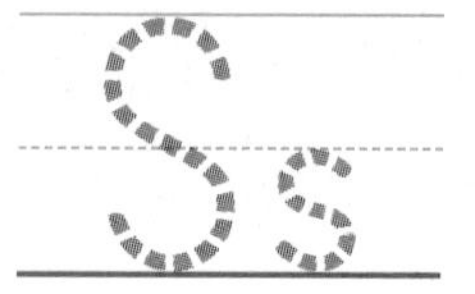

sun

1 s

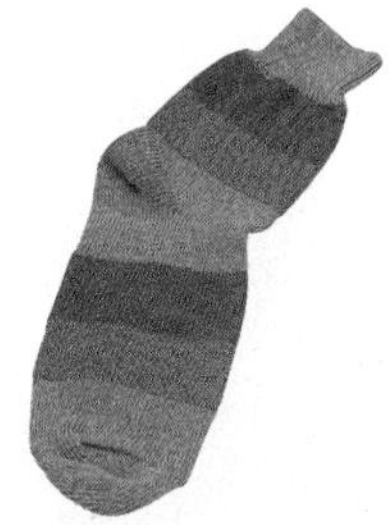

2

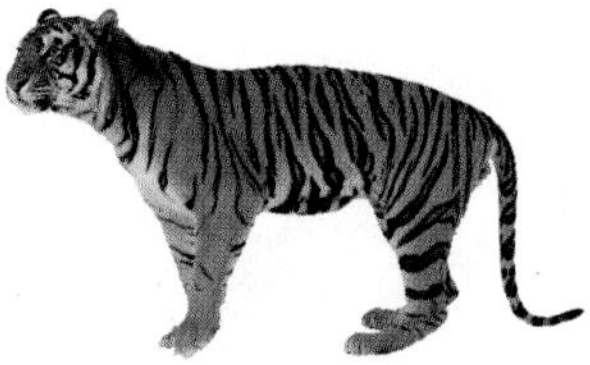

3

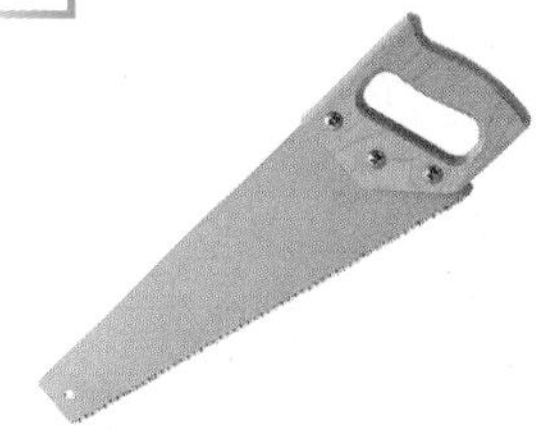

4

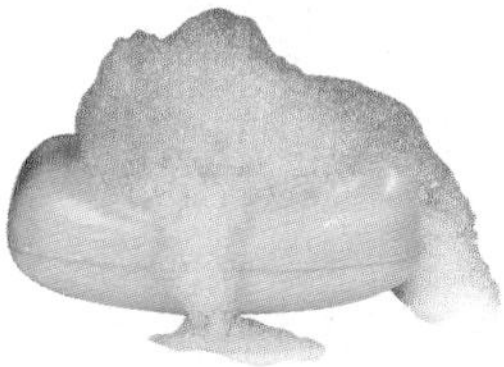

5

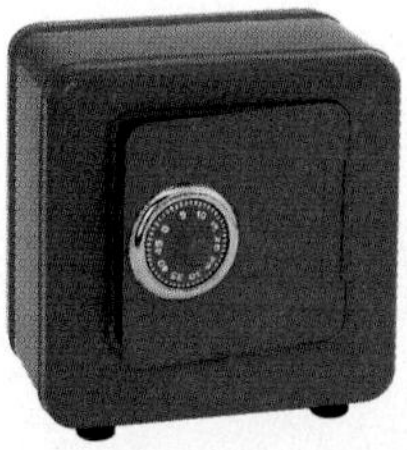

6

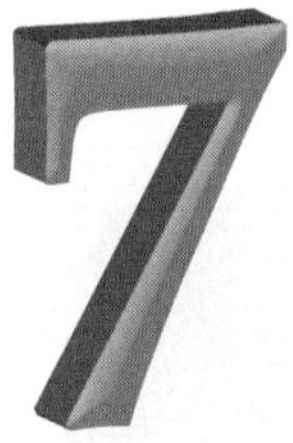

7

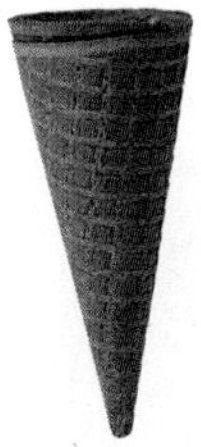

8

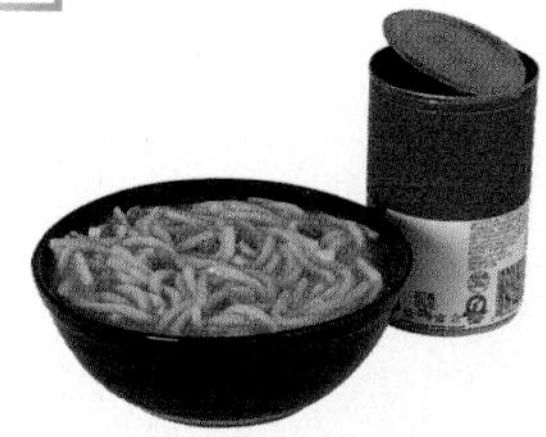

Bus ends with the s sound. Write s if the picture name ends with the s sound.

bus

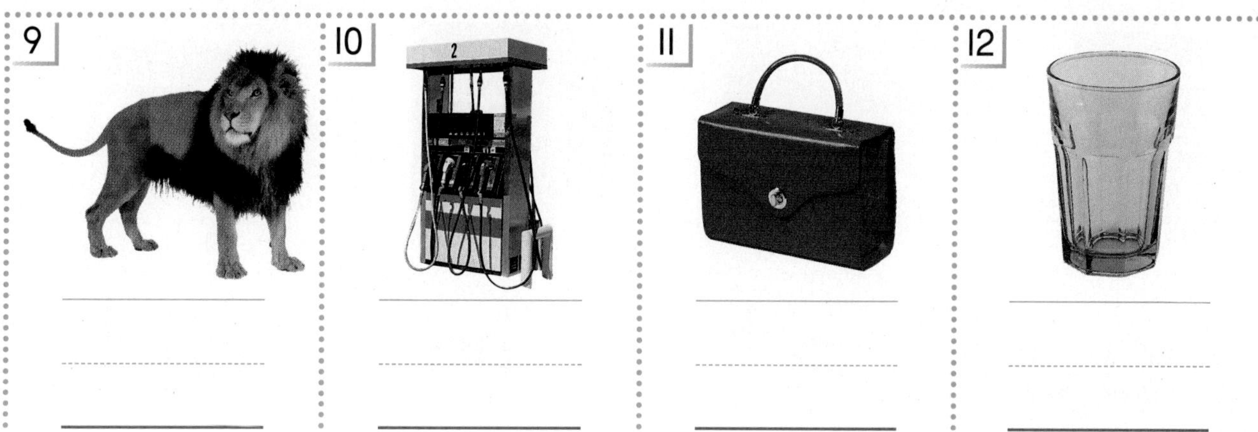

9

10

11

12

Wig begins with the w sound.
Write w if the picture name
begins with the w sound.

1	2	3	4
web	ox	et	ell
5	6	7	8
ag	an	ax	ut
9	10	11	12
ag	et	in	ask

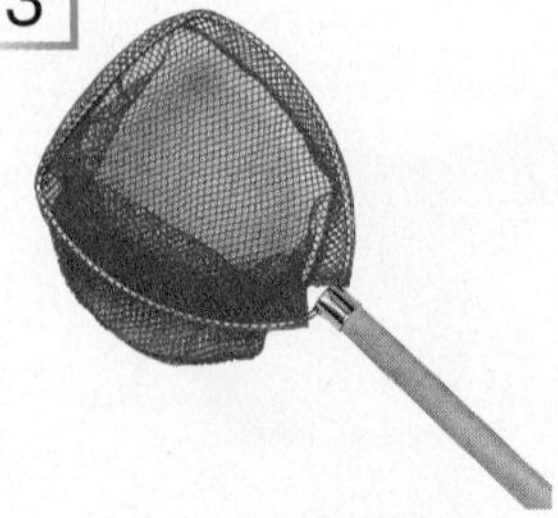

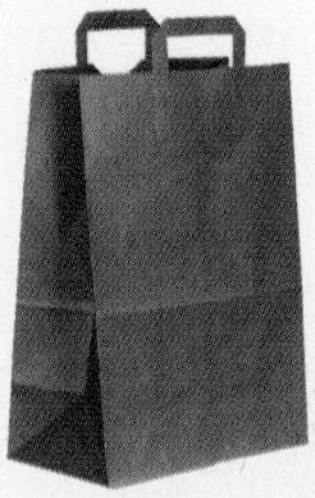

 Name ____________________

k, j, p, n

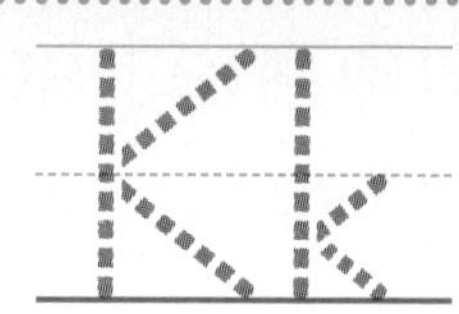

Key begins with the k sound.
Write k if the picture name begins with the k sound.

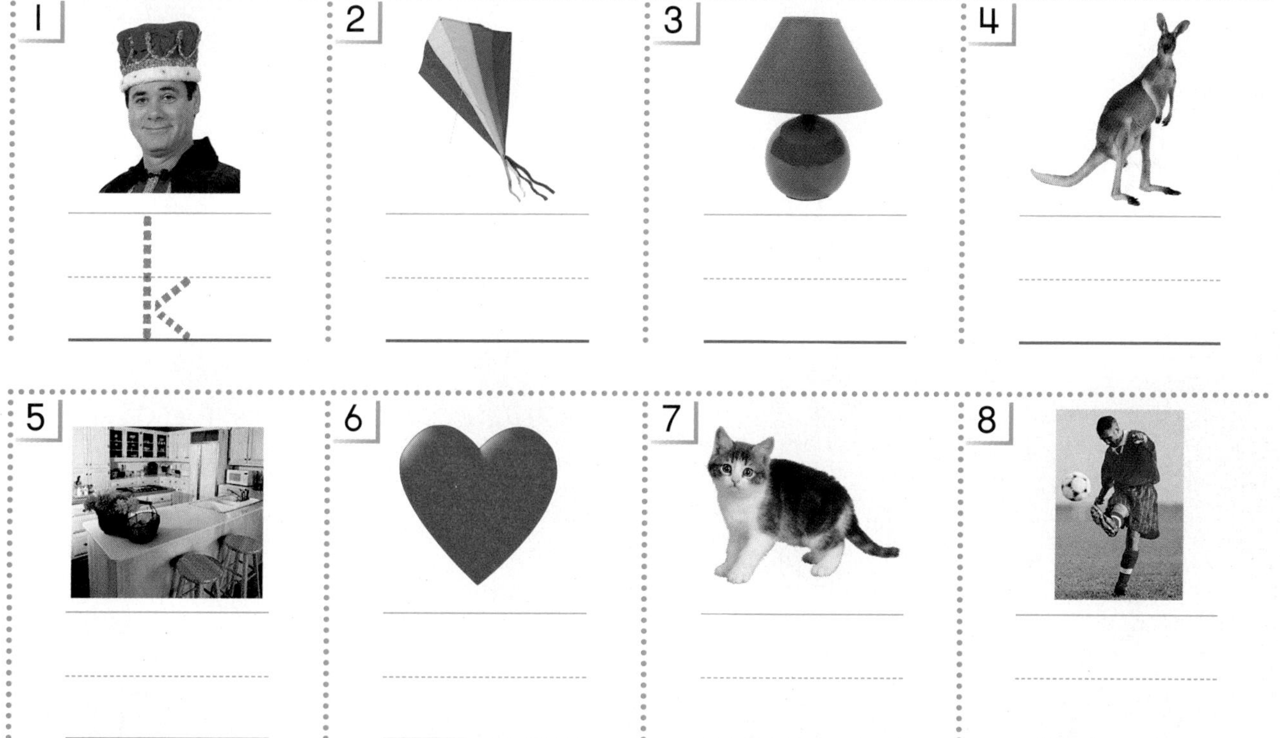

Book ends with the k sound. Write k if the picture name ends with the k sound.

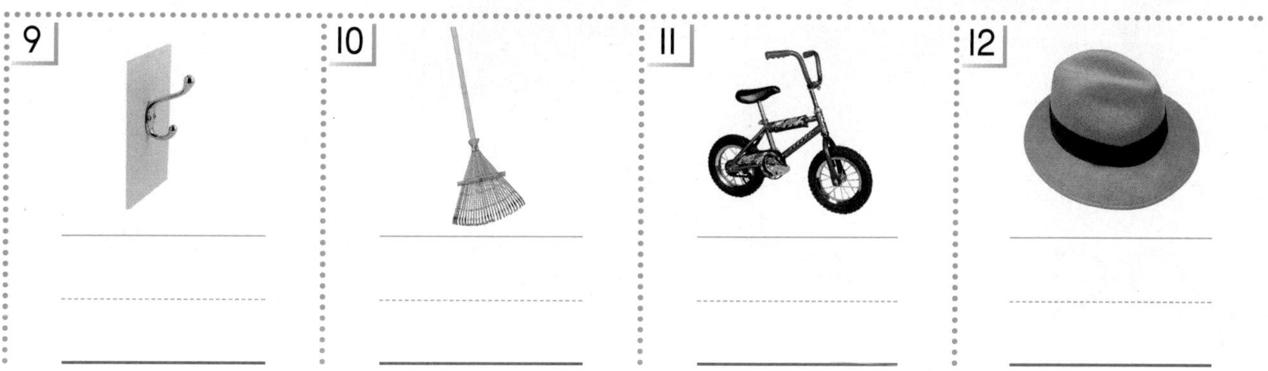

Jam begins with the j sound.
Write j if the picture name
begins with the j sound.

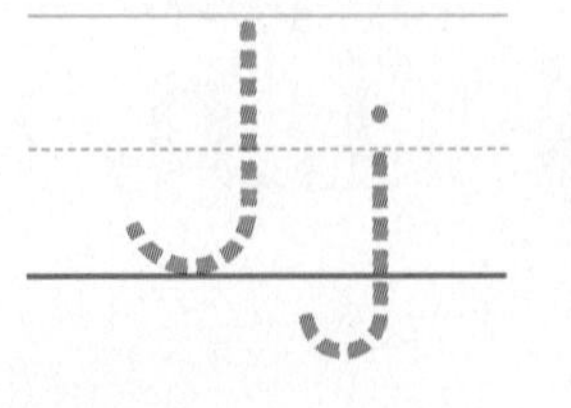

jam

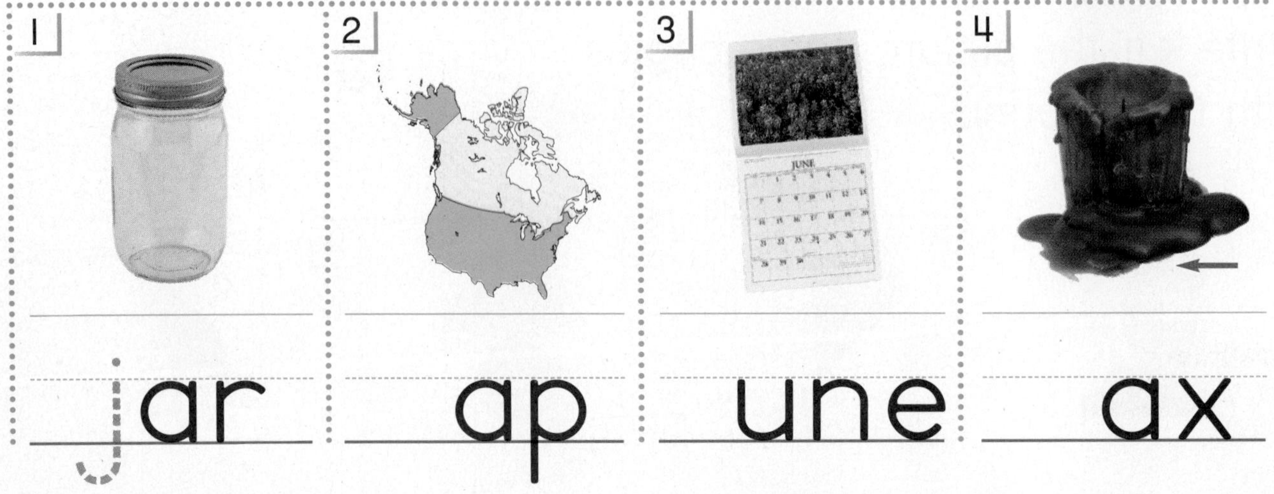

 Name ____________________

Pan begins with the p sound. Write p if the picture name begins with the p sound.

P p

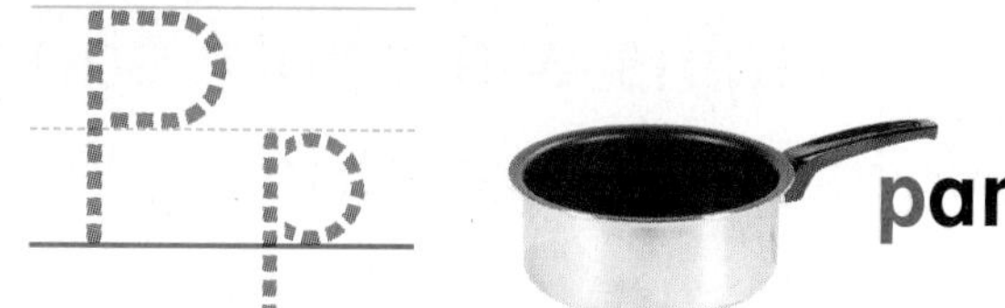

1

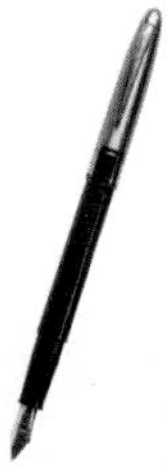

p

2

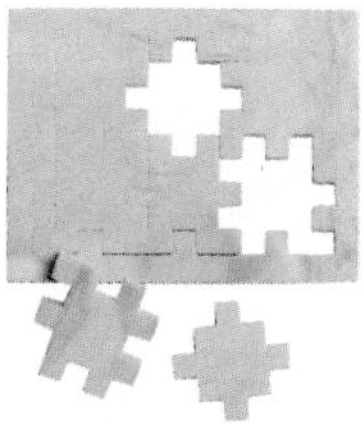

3

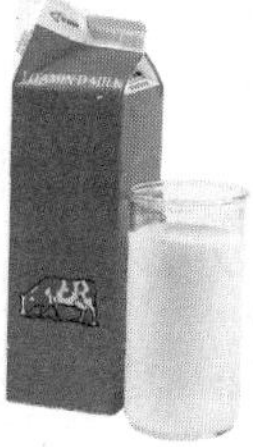

4

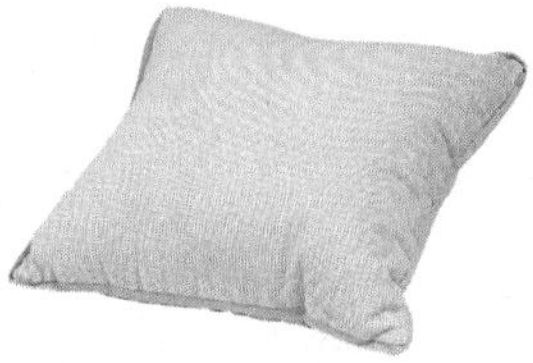

5

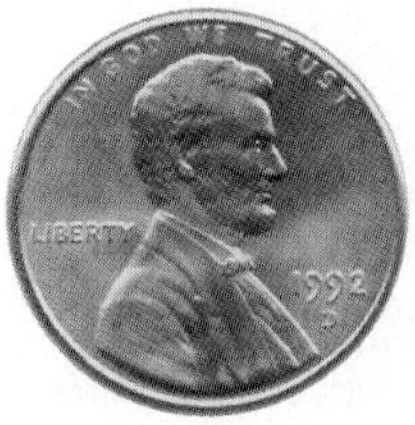

6

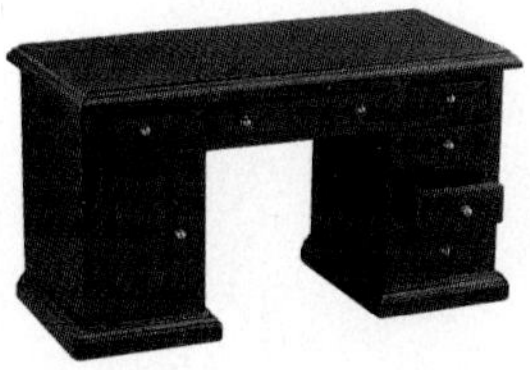

7

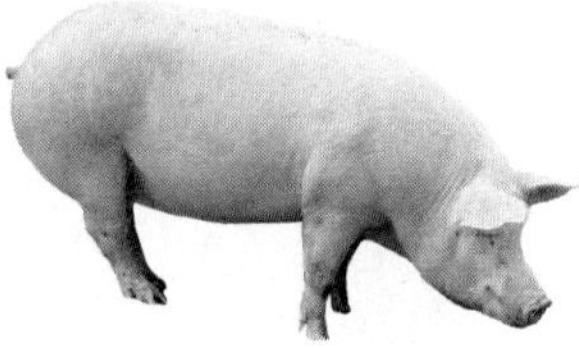

8

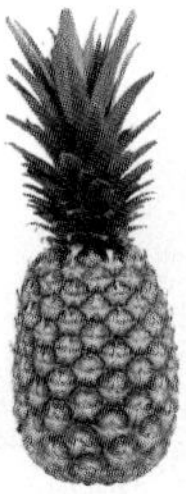

Cup ends with the p sound. Write p if the picture name ends with the p sound.

9

10

11

12

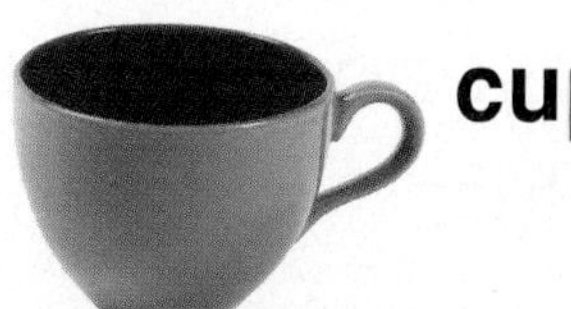

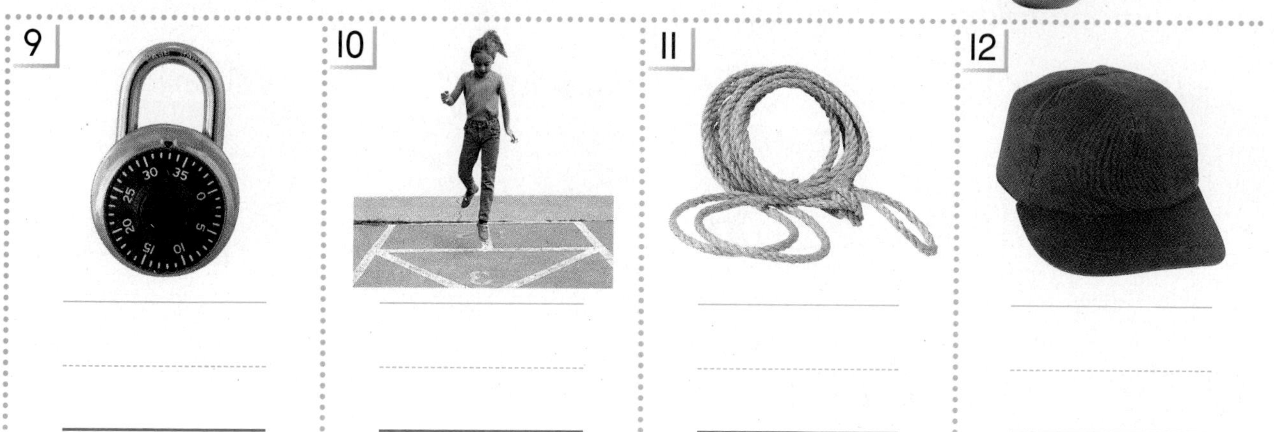

Nut begins with the n sound.
Write n if the picture name
begins with the n sound.

Nn

nut

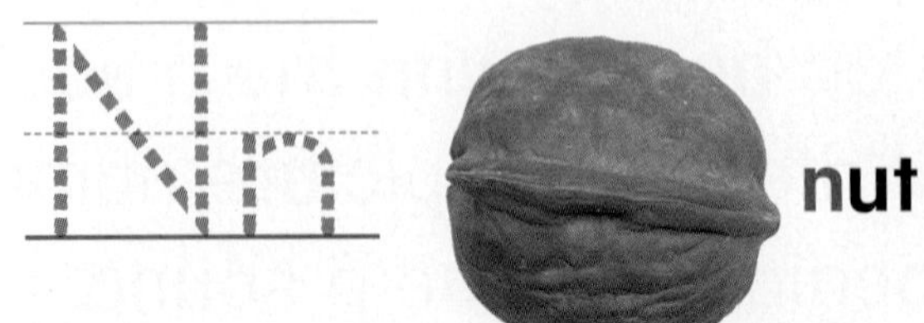

1

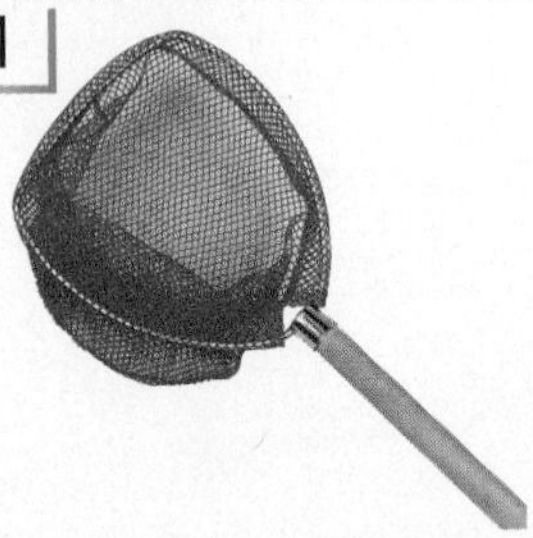

net

2

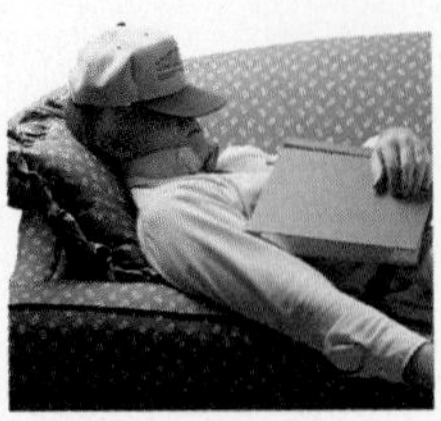

ap

3

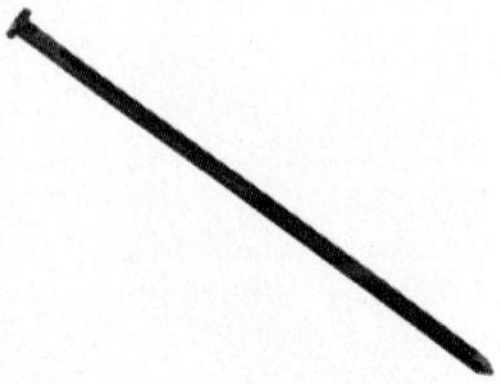

ail

4

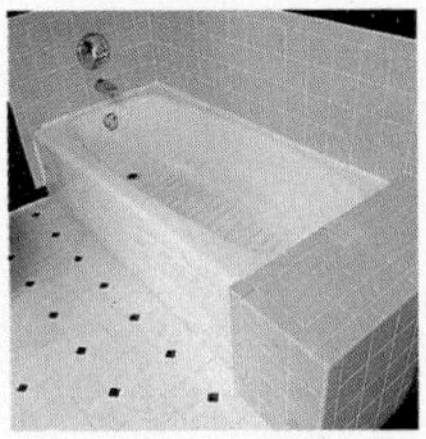

ub

5

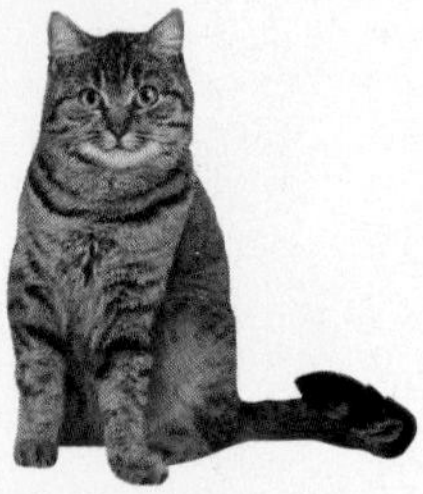

at

6

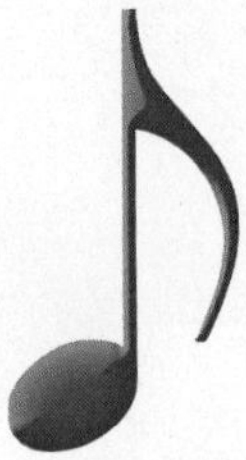

ote

7

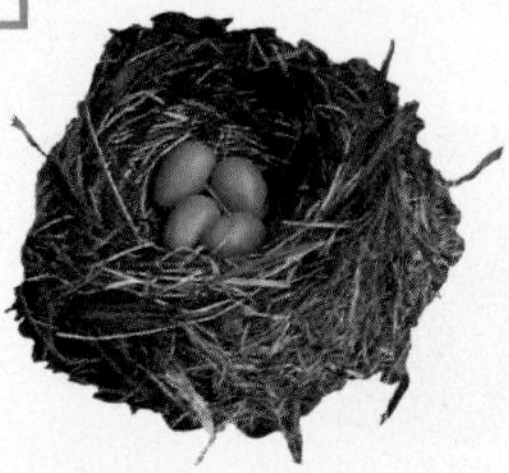

est

8

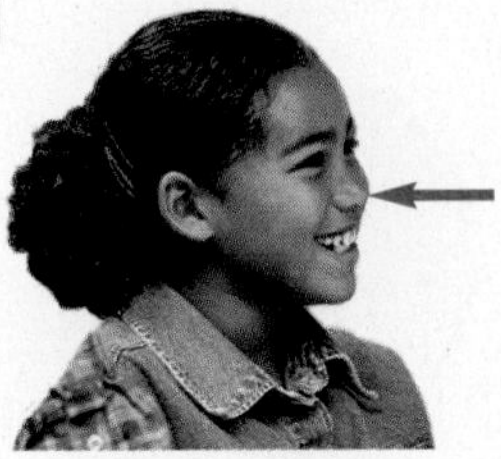

ose

Can ends with the n sound. Write n if the
picture name ends with the n sound.

can

9

va

10

pi

11

su

12

ca

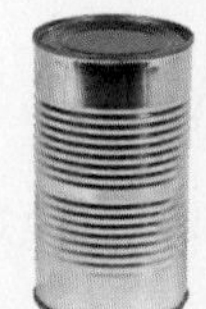

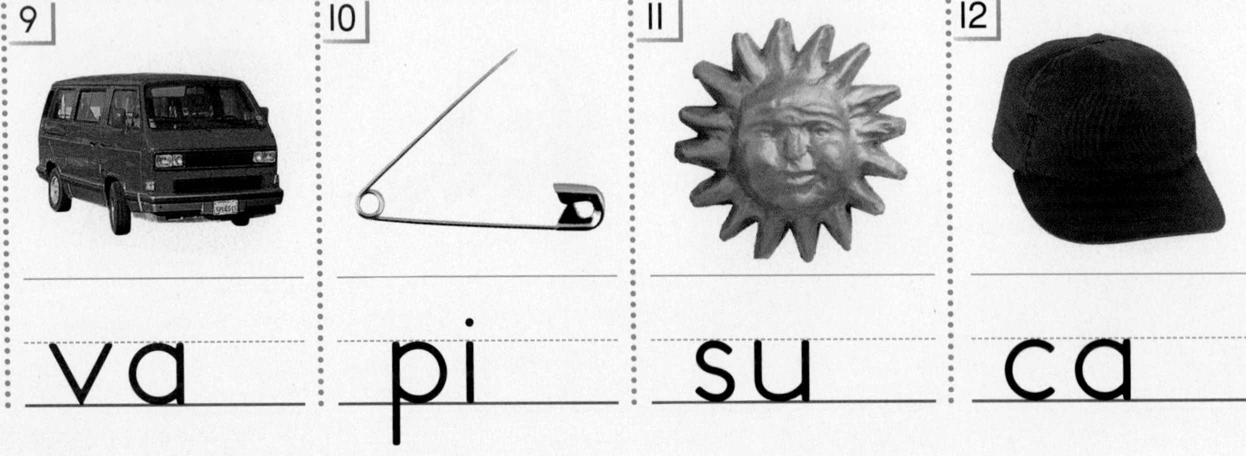

 Name ______________________________

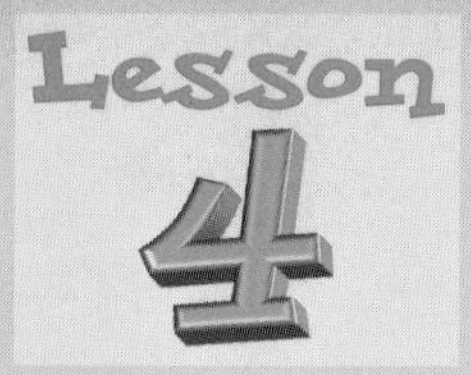

Lesson 4 c, h, l, r

Cat begins with the c sound.
Write c if the picture name begins
with the c sound.

cat

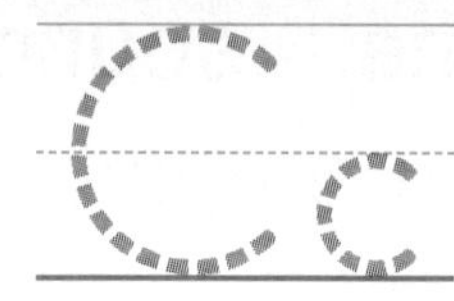

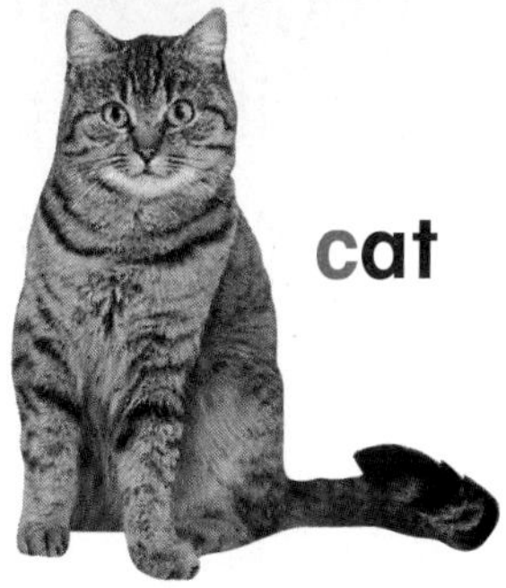

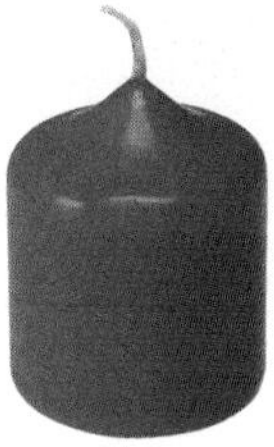

1
c

2

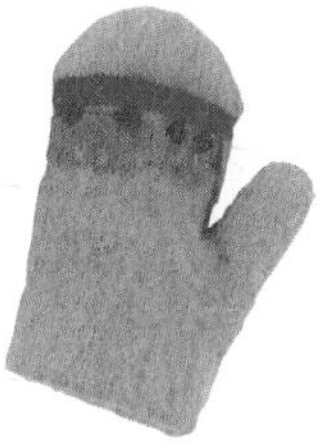

3

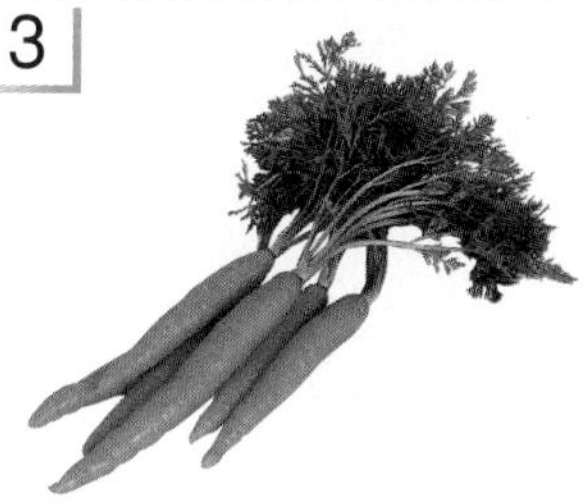

4

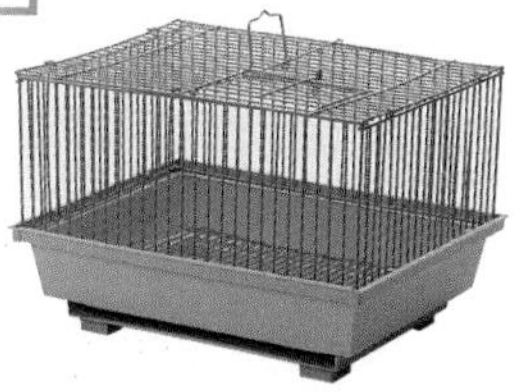

5

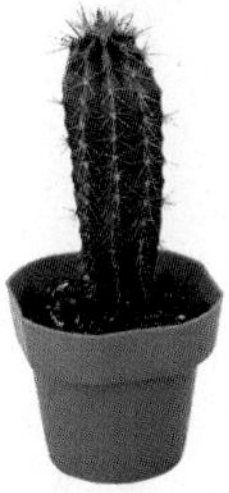

6

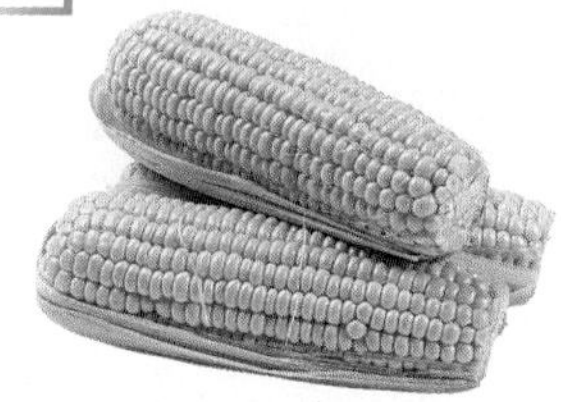

7

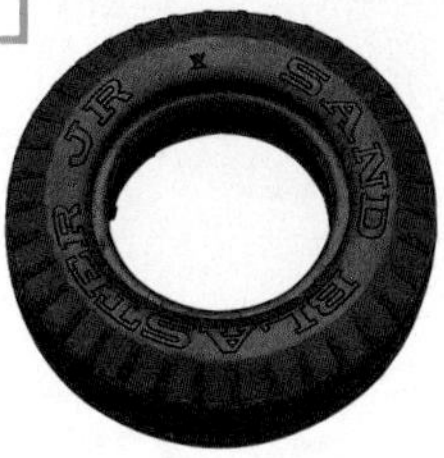

8

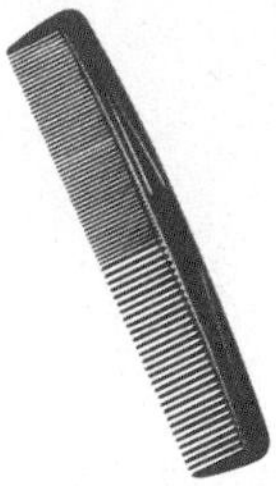

9

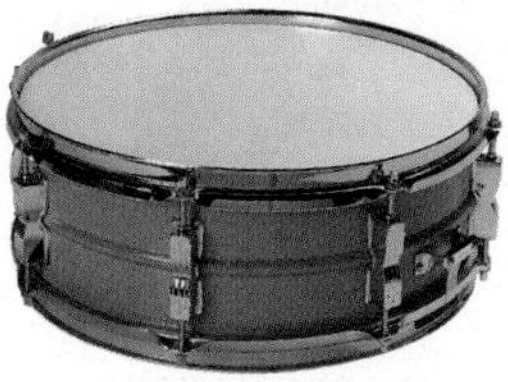

10

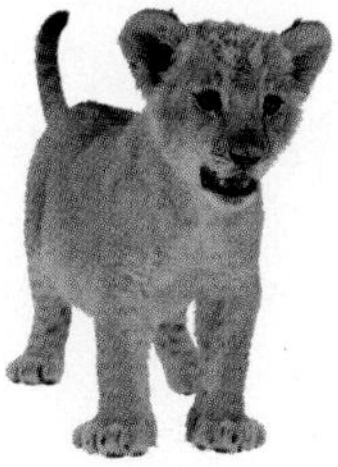

11

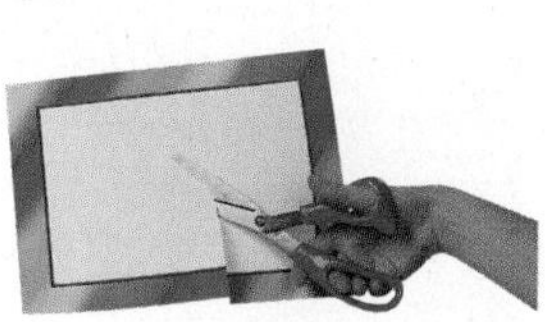

12

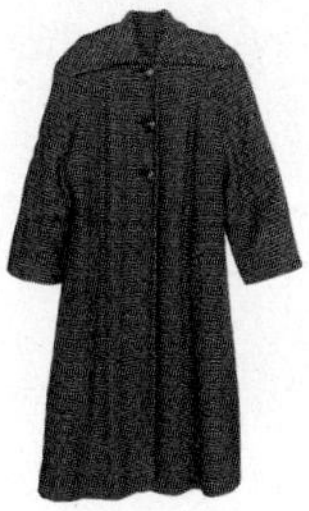

Hat begins with the h sound.
Write h if the picture name
begins with the h sound.

Hh

hat

1
ham

2
en

3
ot

4
and

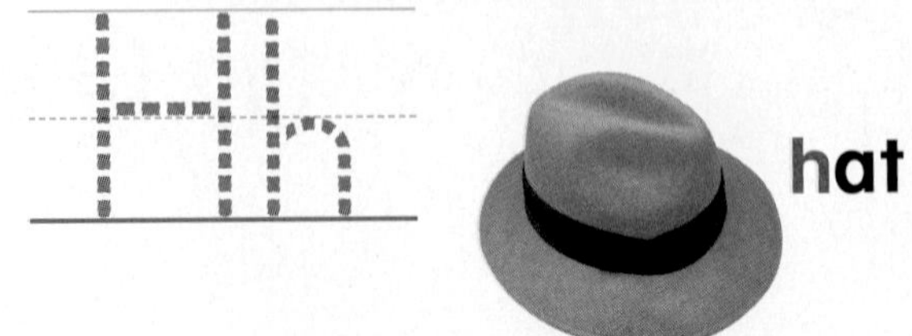

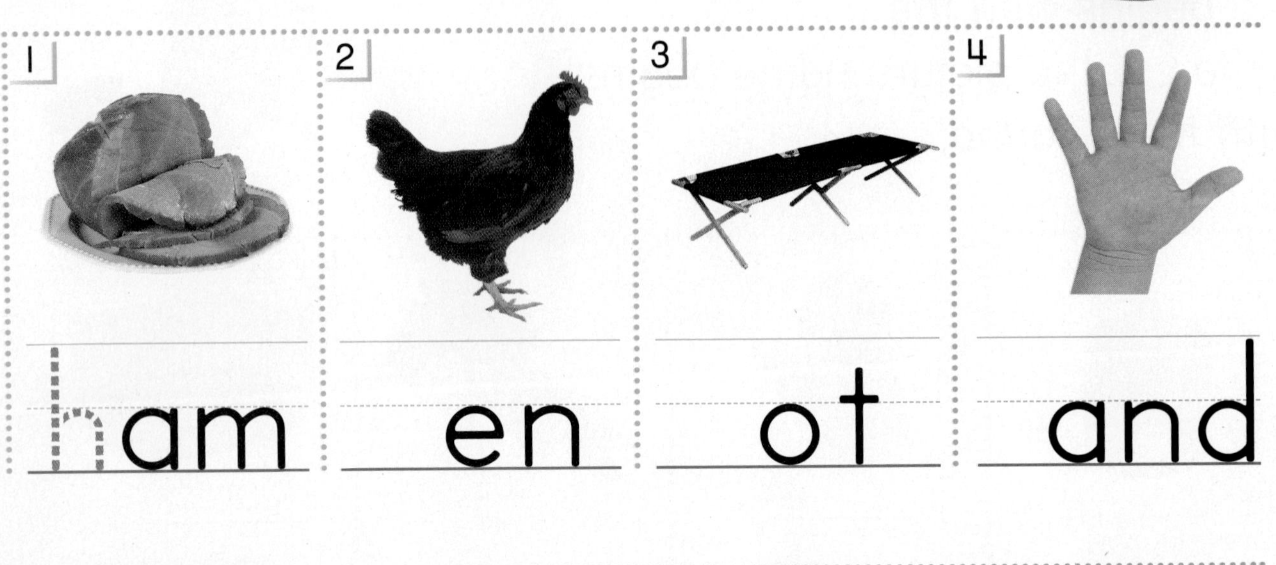

5 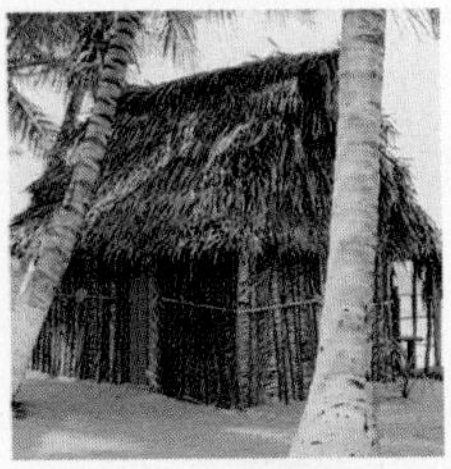
ut

6 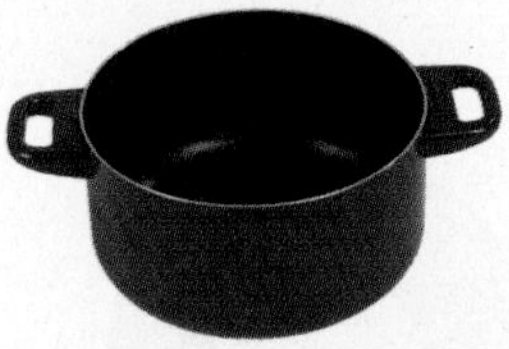
ot

7 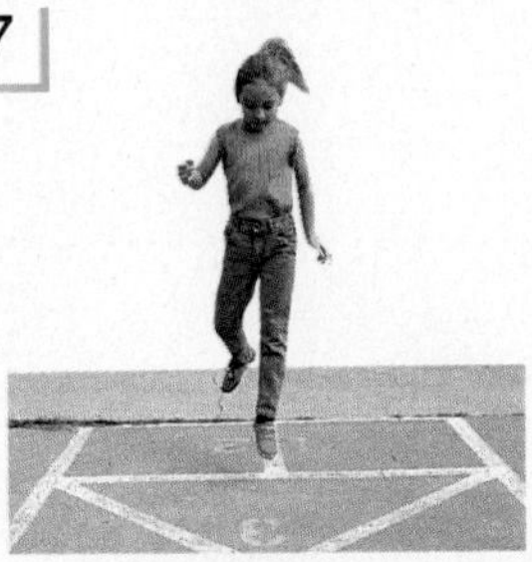
op

8 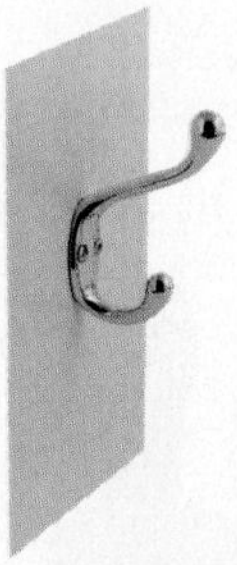
ook

9 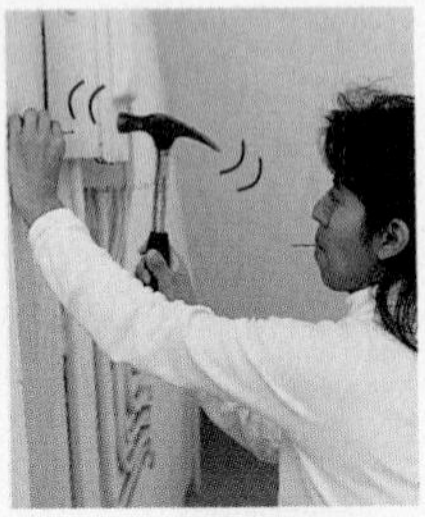
it

10 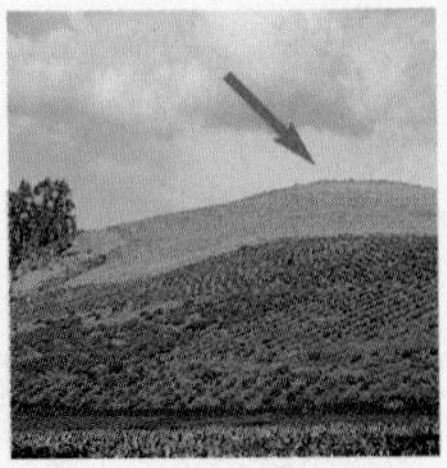
ill

11 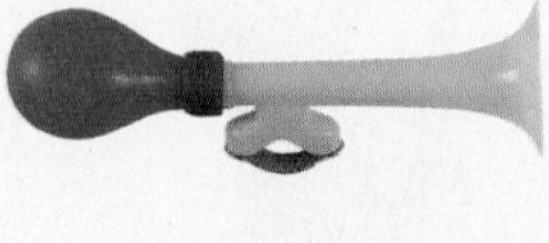
orn

12 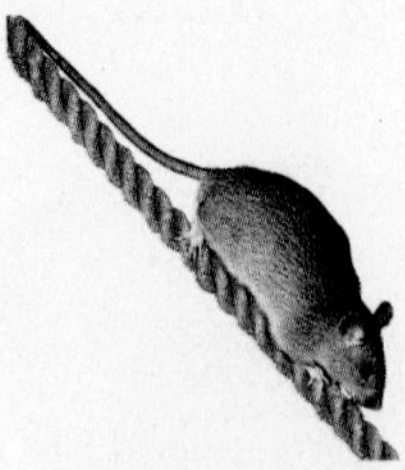
at

Name ______

Lamp begins with the l sound.
Write l if the picture name
begins with the l sound.

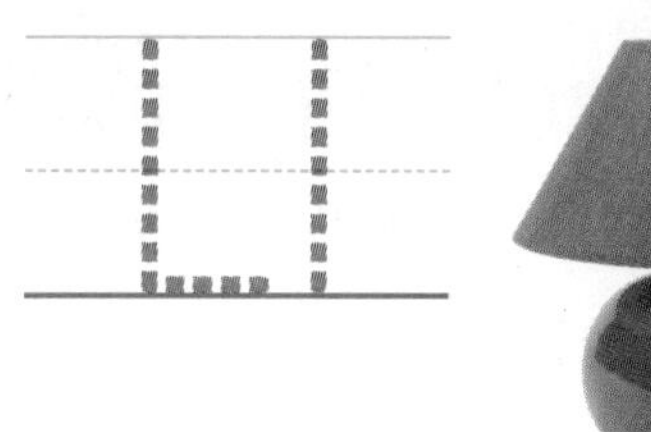

lamp

1

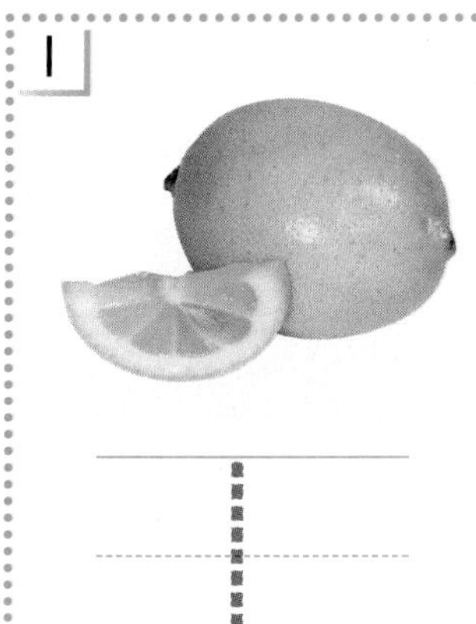

2

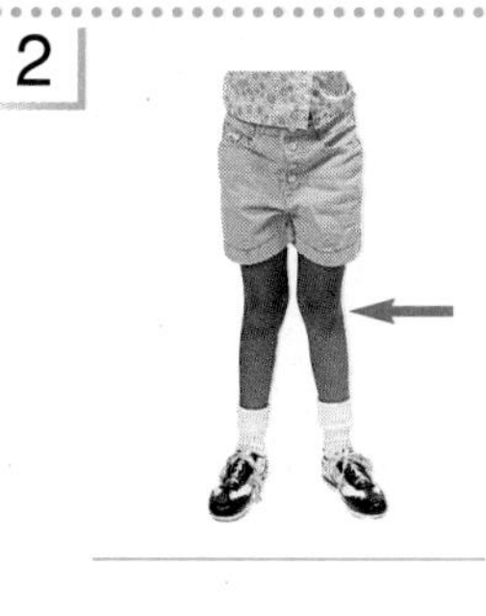

3

4

5

6

7

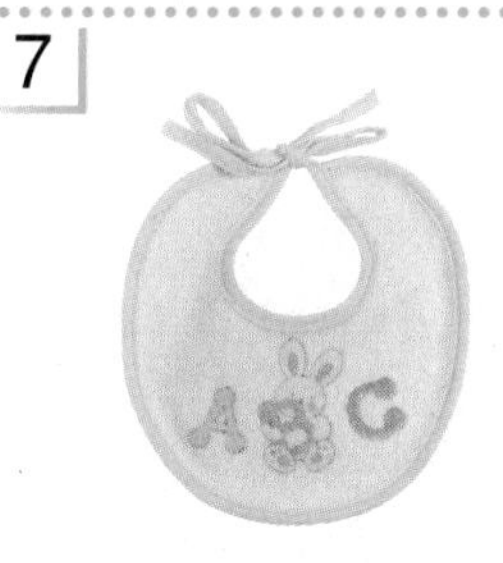

8

Mail ends with the l sound. Write l if
the picture name ends with the l sound.

mail

9

10

11

12

Rug begins with the r sound. Write r if the picture name begins with the r sound.

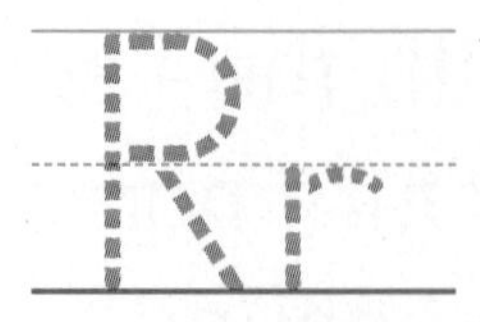

rug

1	2	3	4
r un	at	at	ock

5	6	7	8
at	ed	ake	ose

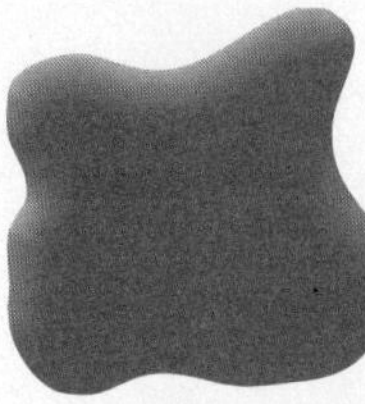

Car ends with the r sound. Write r if the picture name ends with the r sound.

car

9	10	11	12
ja	be	sta	fou

Name ______________________

v, y, z, qu, x

Vest begins with the v sound.
Write v if the picture name begins with the v sound.

1  v

2 

3 

4 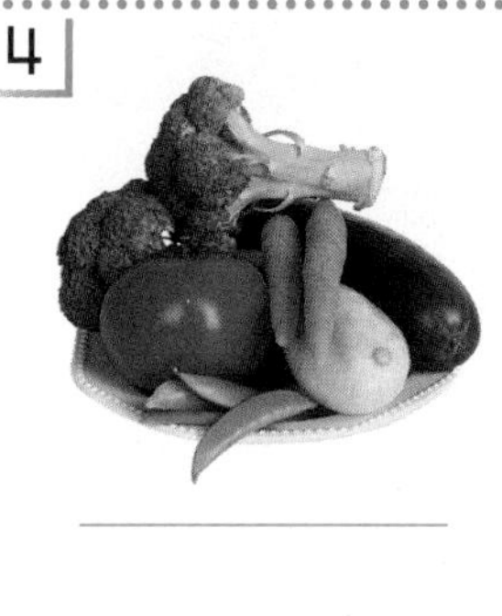

5 

6 

7 

8 

9 10

10 

11 

12 

Yam begins with the y sound.
Write y if the picture name
begins with the y sound.

Y y

yam

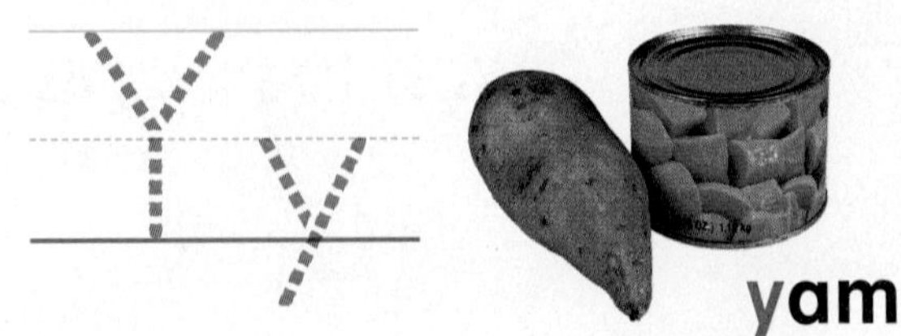

1

yell

2

_at

3

_arn

4

_ed

5

_ard

6

_ag

7

_olk

8

_ig

9

_og

10

_awn

11

_in

12

_ellow

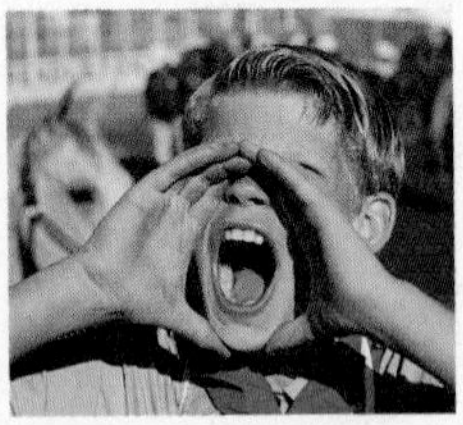

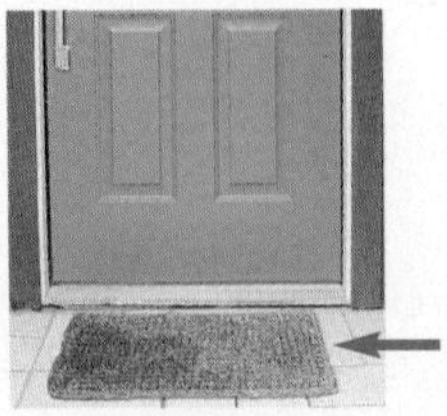

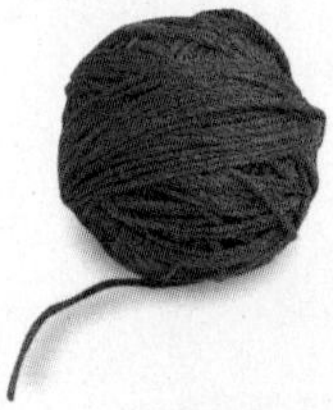

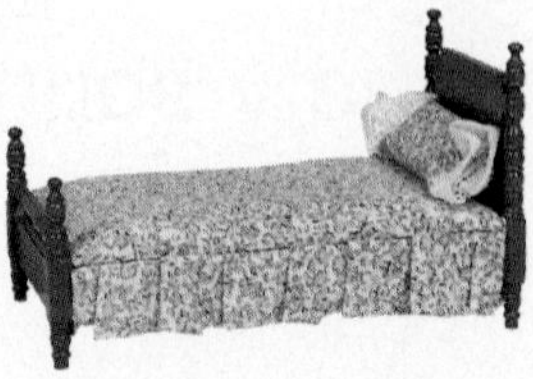

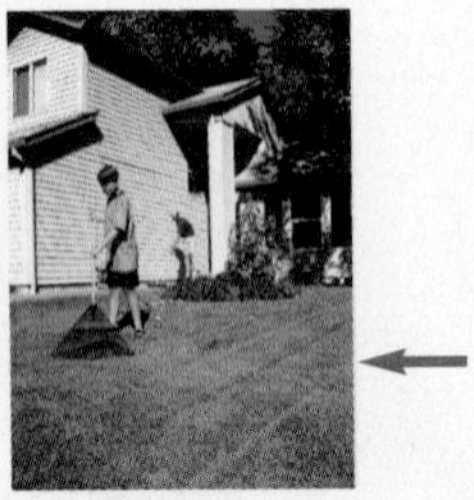

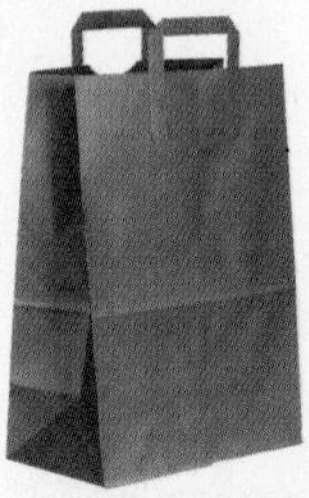

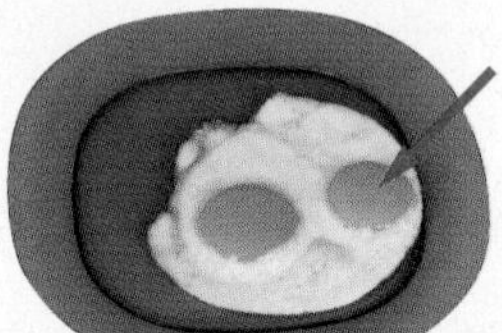

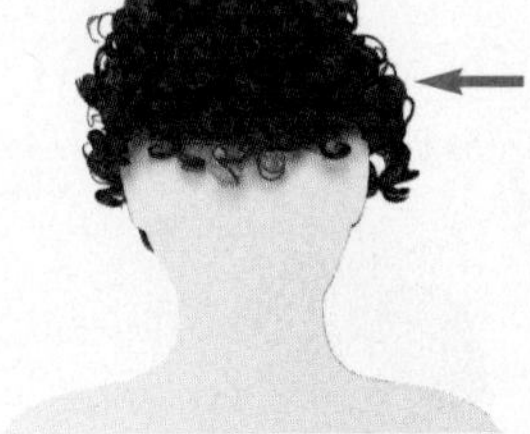

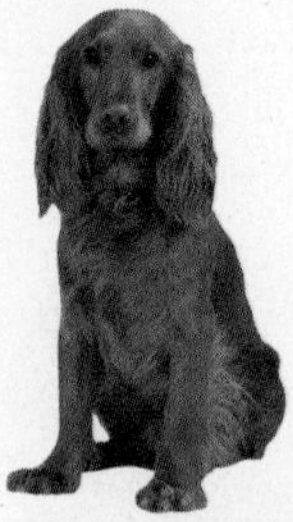

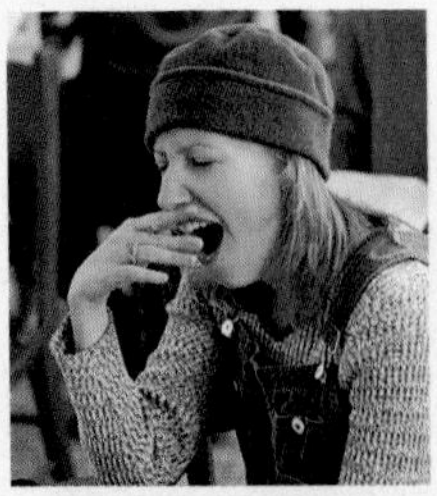

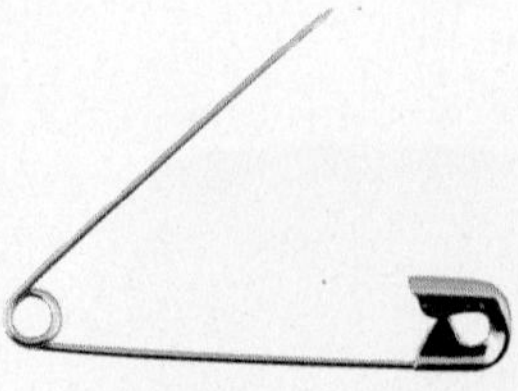

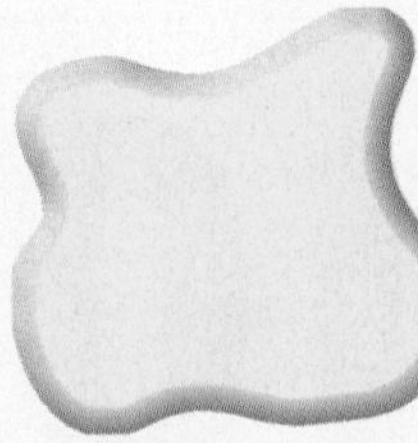

Name ________________________

Zip begins with the z sound.
Write z if the picture name begins with the z sound.

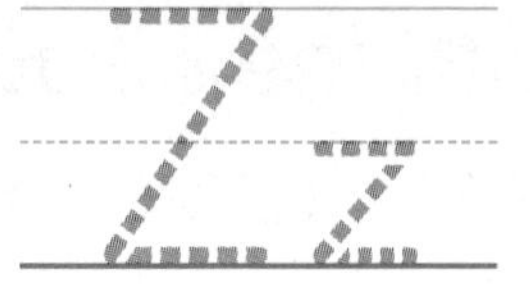

zip

1

z

2

3

4
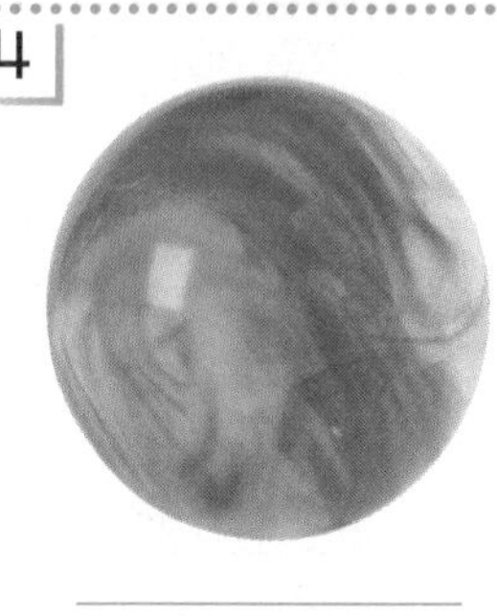

5

6

7

8

9

10

11

12

Quilt begins with the qu sound. Write qu if the picture name begins with the qu sound.

quilt

1  queen

2  og

3  art

4  est

5  ack

6  ail

Six ends with the x sound. Write x if the picture name ends with the x sound.

six

7

bu

8

bo

9

mi

10

a

 Name ____________________

Unit 1 Review

Lessons 1–5

Write the letter that stands for the first sound in each picture name.

m d f g b t s w k j

1

2

3

4

5

6

7

8

9

10

11

12

Write the letter that stands for the first sound in each picture name.

p n c h l r v y z qu

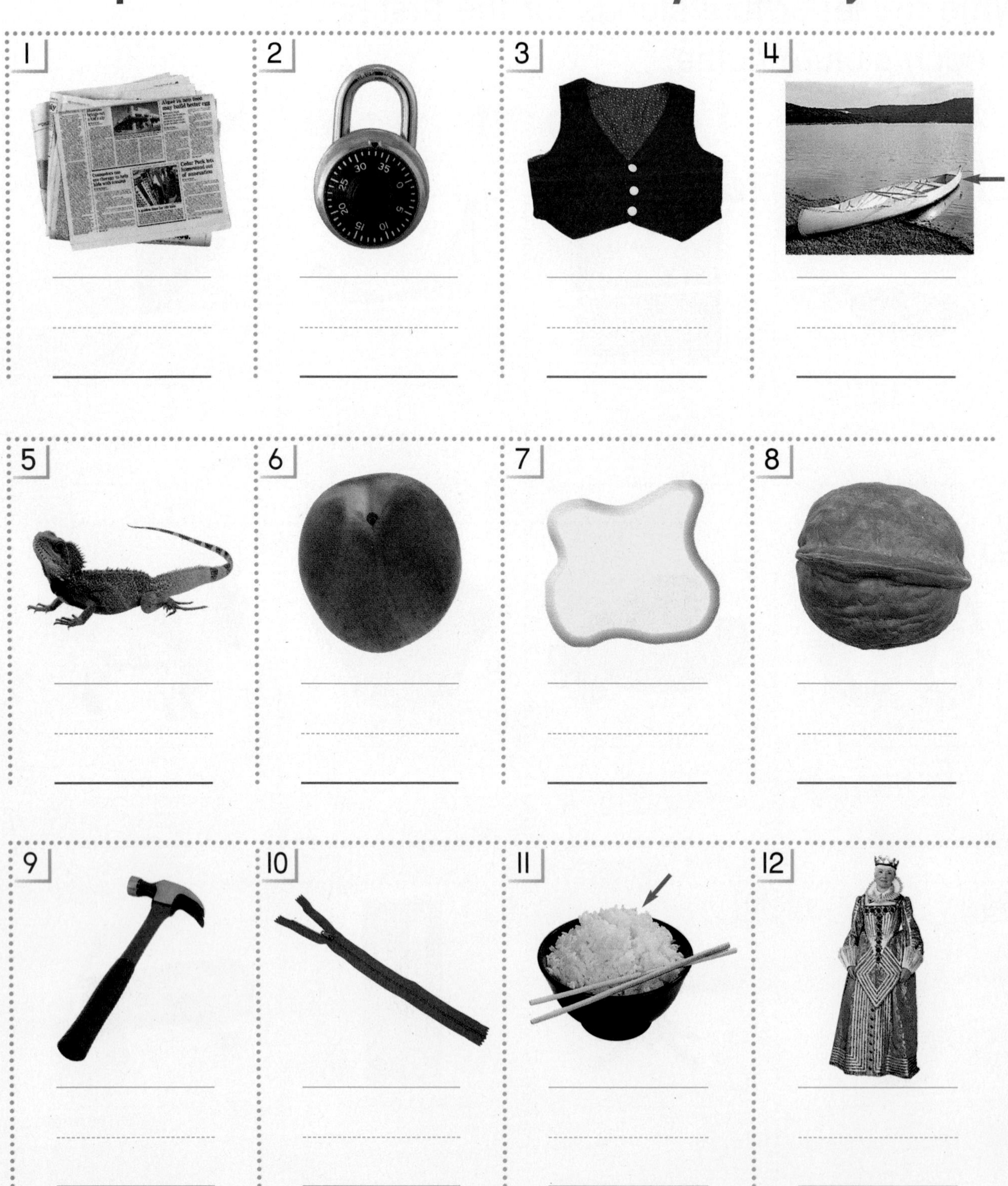

 Name ____________________

Circle the letter that stands for the last sound in each picture name. Then write the letter.

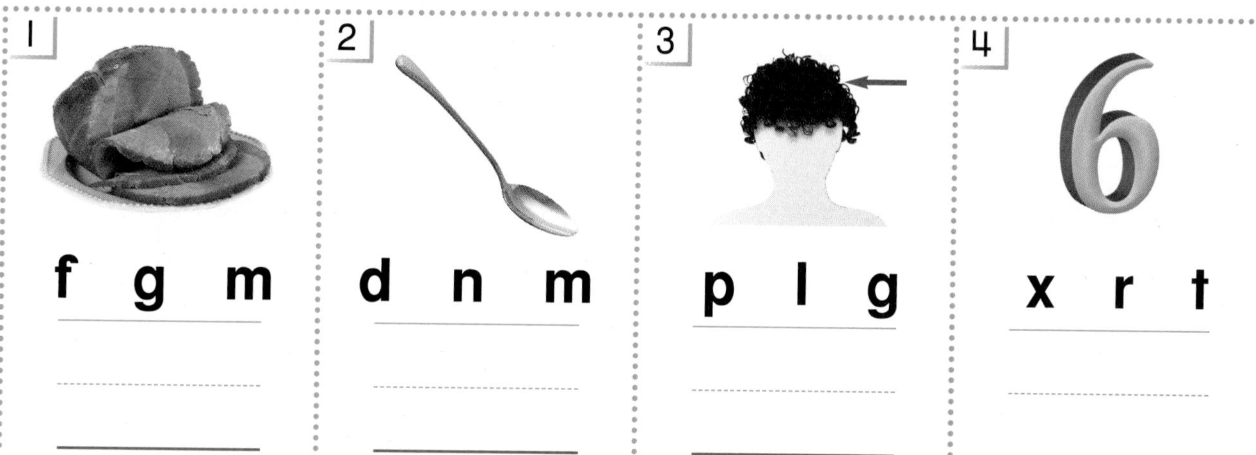

1. f g m
2. d n m
3. p l g
4. x r t

5. h p l
6. f l x
7. d k t
8. p b g

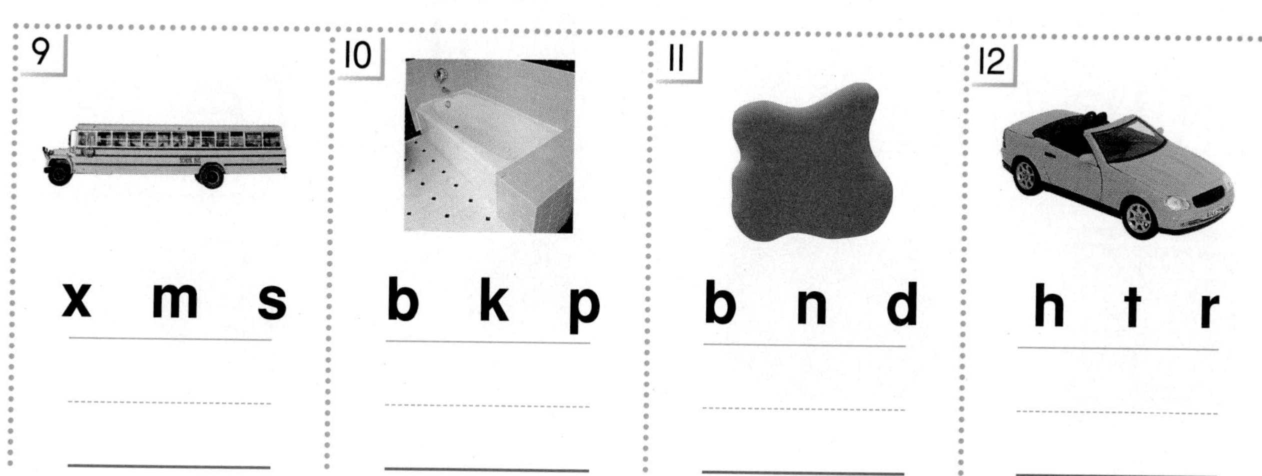

9. x m s
10. b k p
11. b n d
12. h t r

Write the missing letter or letters to complete each word.

m d h s w qu t

n v g p r x y z

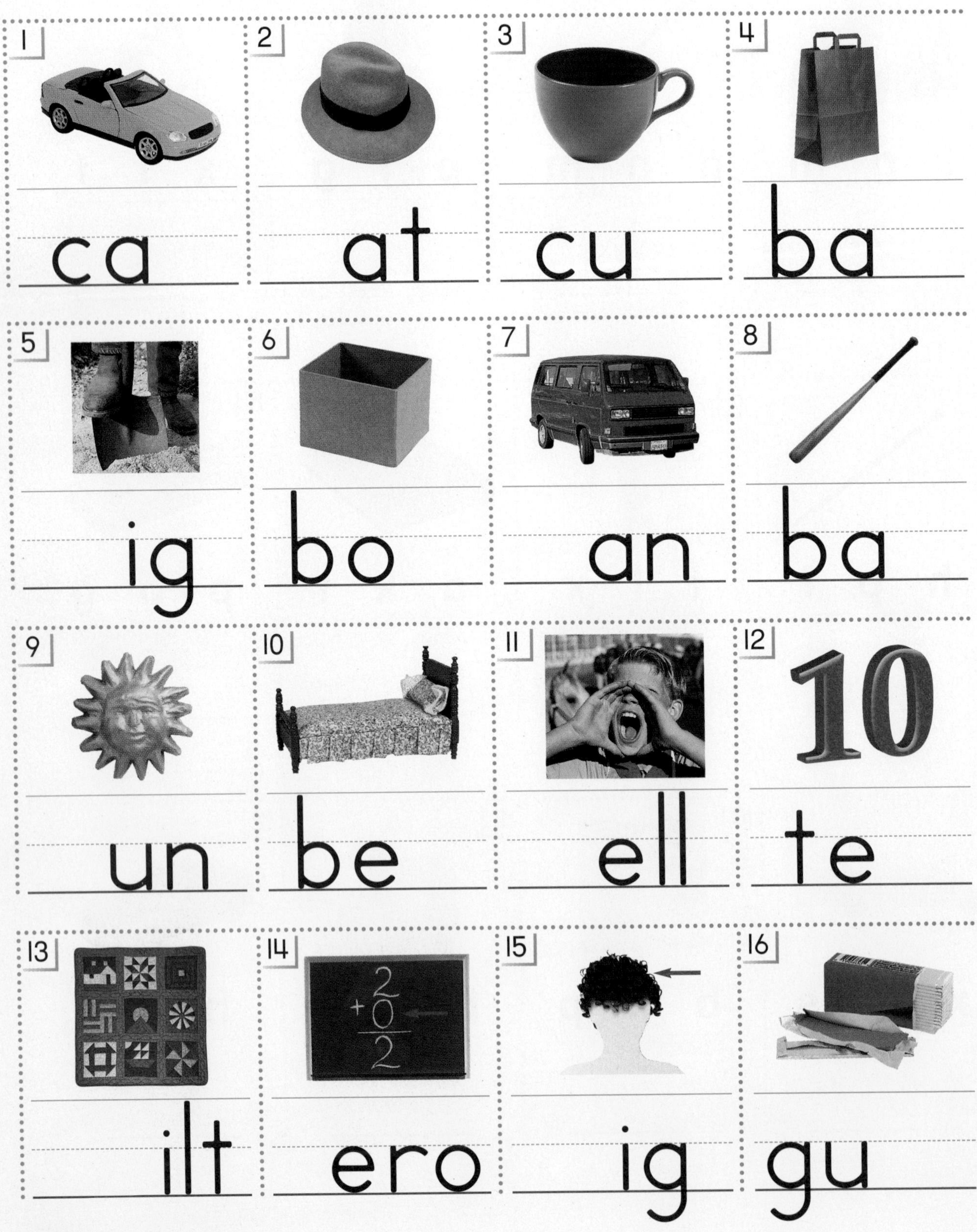

 Name ______

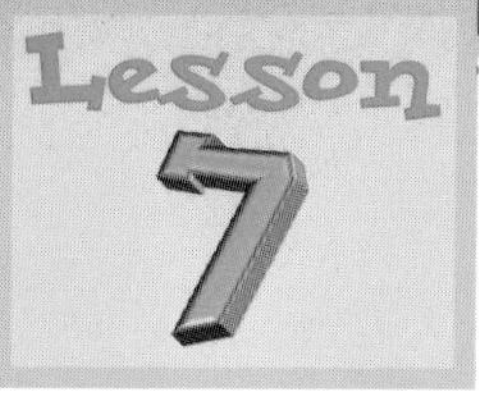

Lesson 7 Short a

Aa

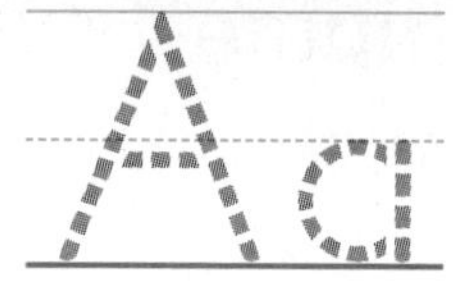

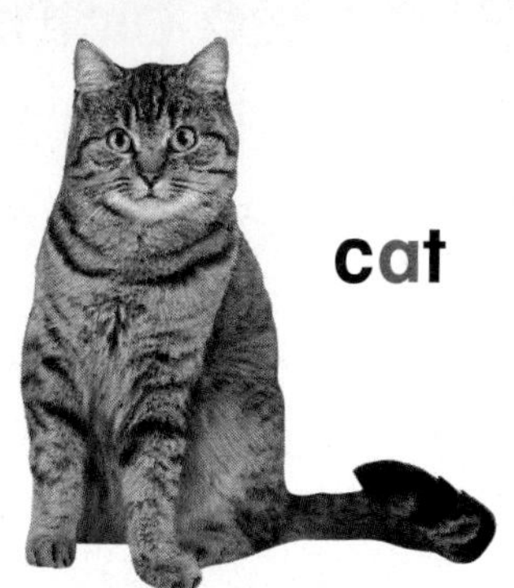

cat

Cat has the short a sound.
Say each picture name.
Write a if you hear the short a sound.

1

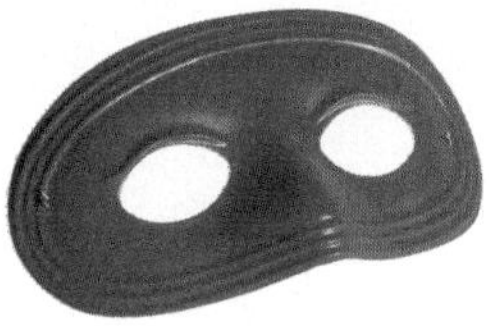

a

2

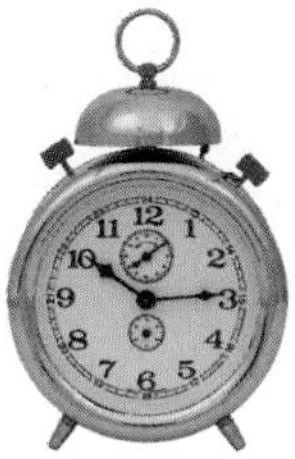

3

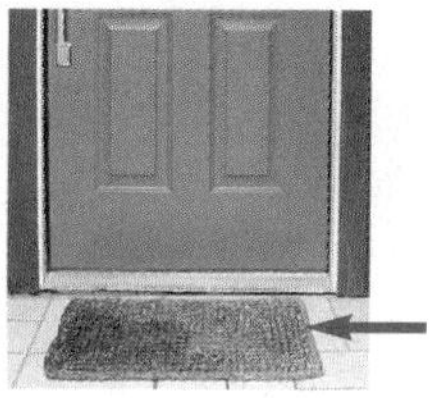

4

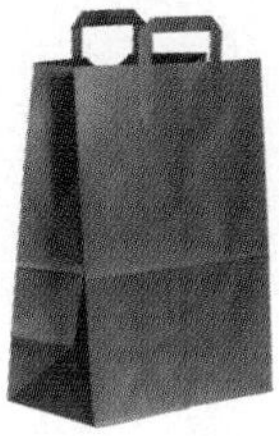

5

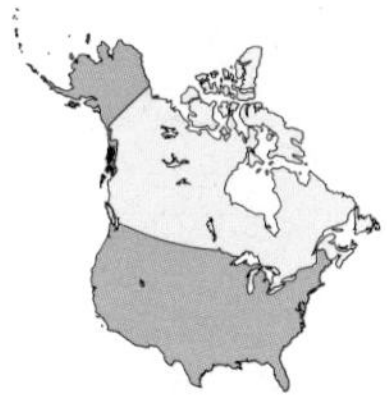

6

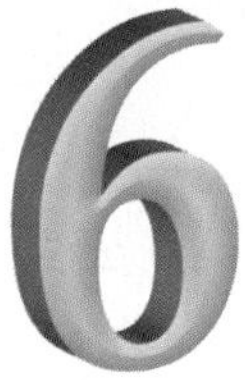

7

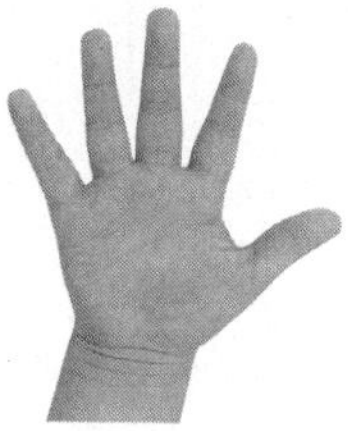

8

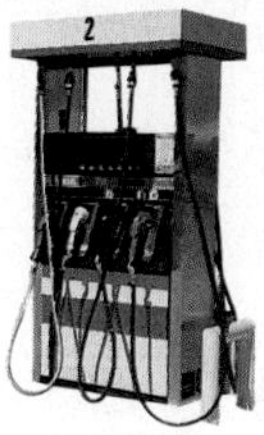

9

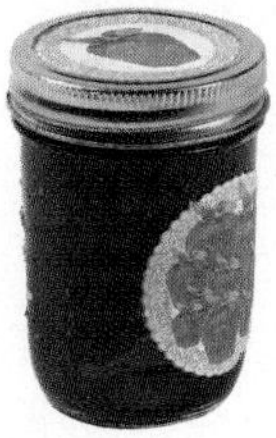

10

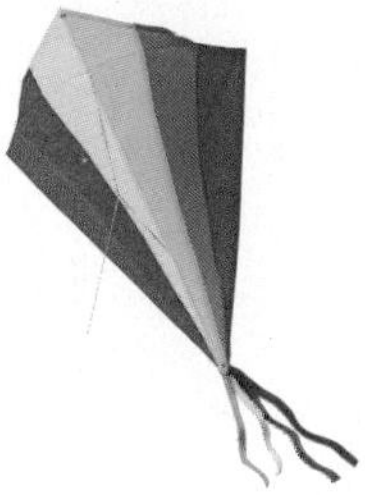

11

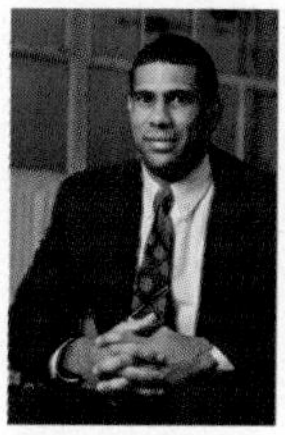

12

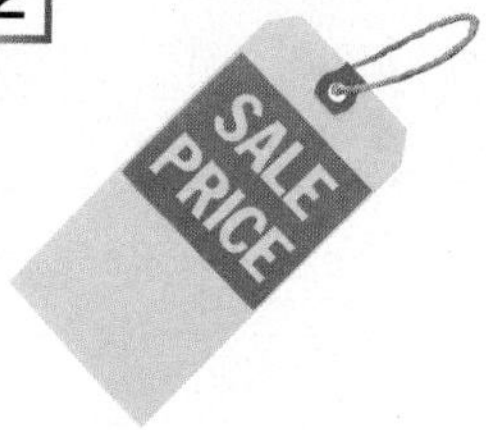

Say each picture name.
Write a if you hear the short a sound.
Color each short a picture.

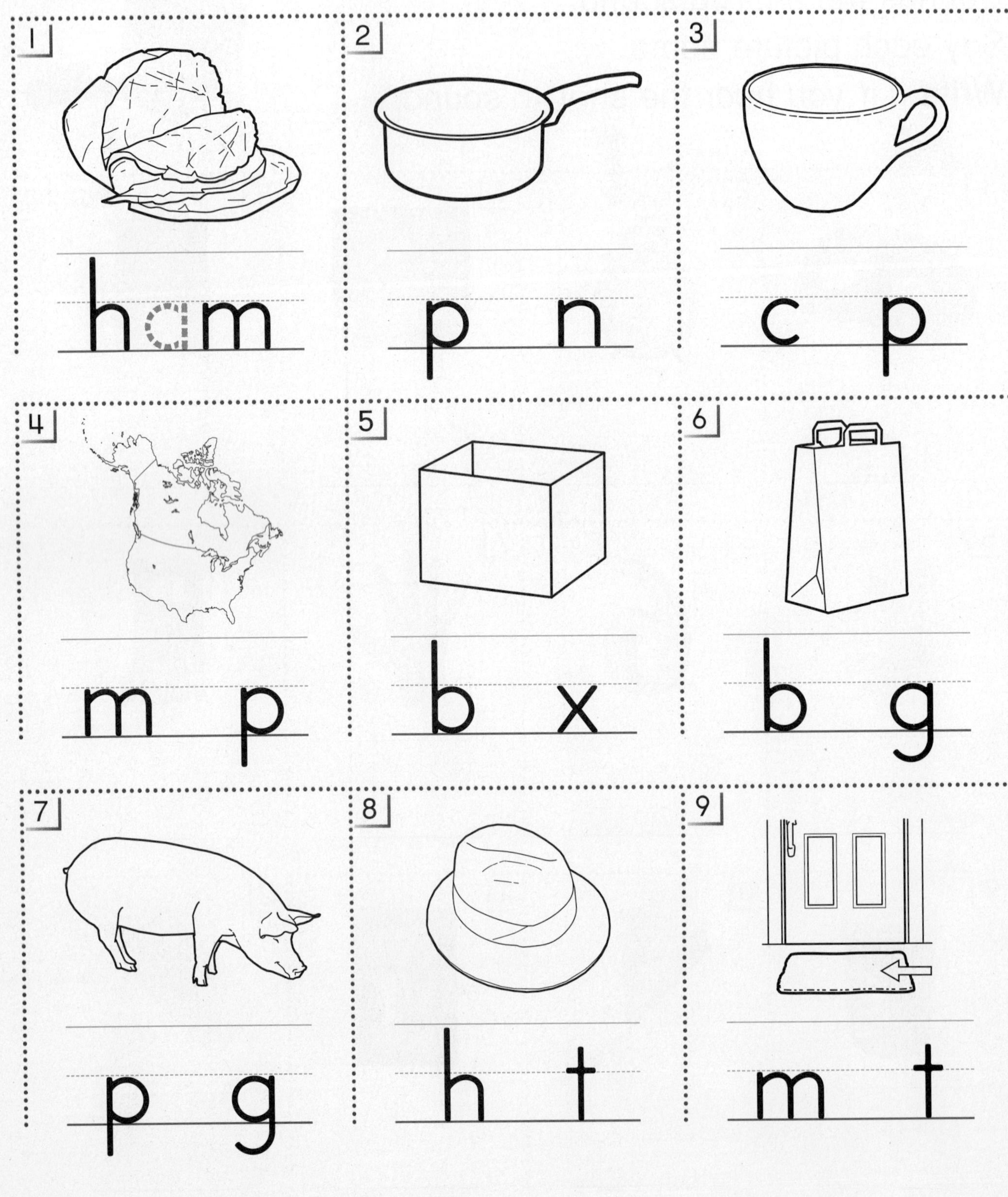

 Name ____________________

Say the word that names the first picture. Circle the pictures whose names rhyme with the word.

Say each picture name. Trace the first letter.
Then write an to make the word.

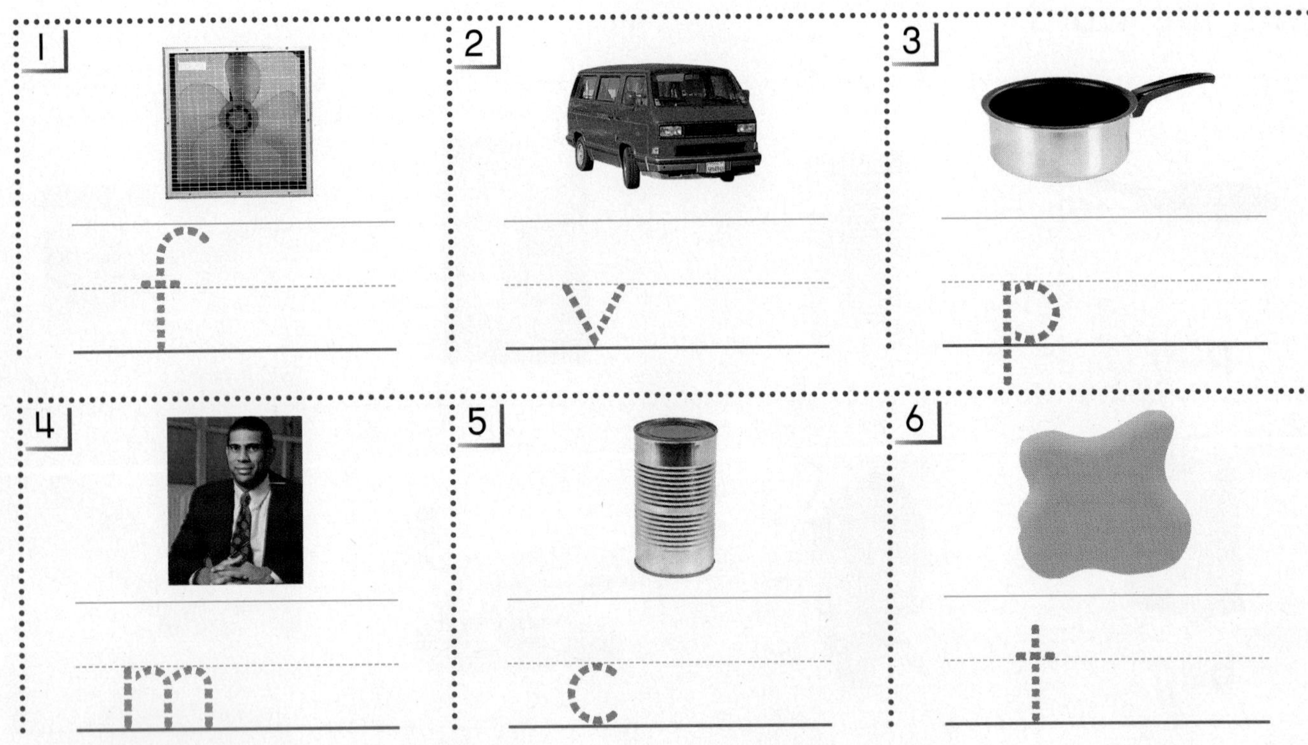

Say each picture name. Trace the first letter.
Then write at to make the word.

Name ____________________

Short e

Bed has the short e sound.
Say each picture name.
Write e if you hear the short e sound.

bed

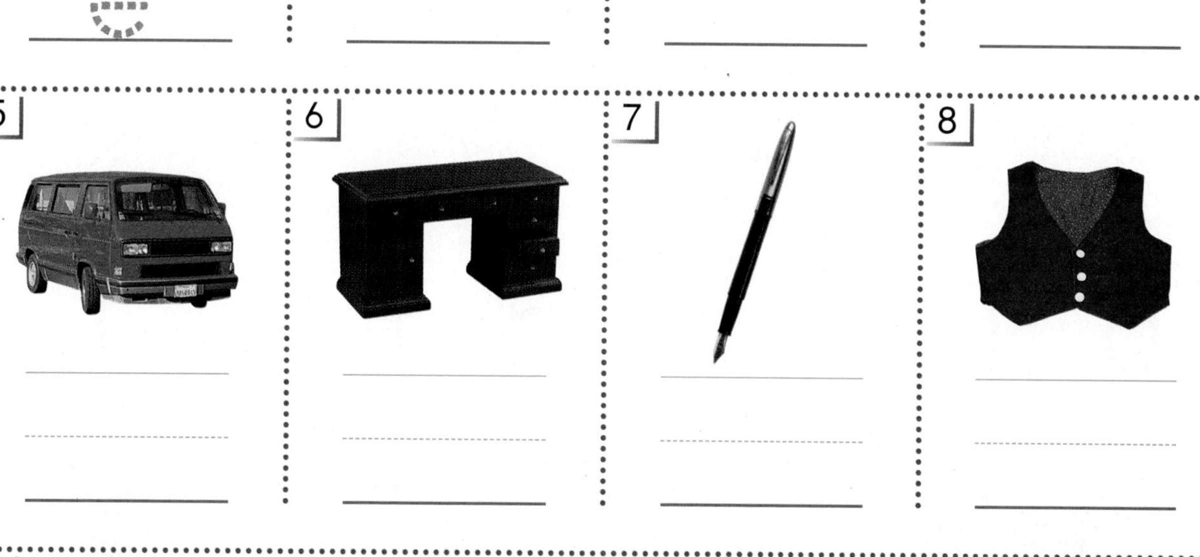

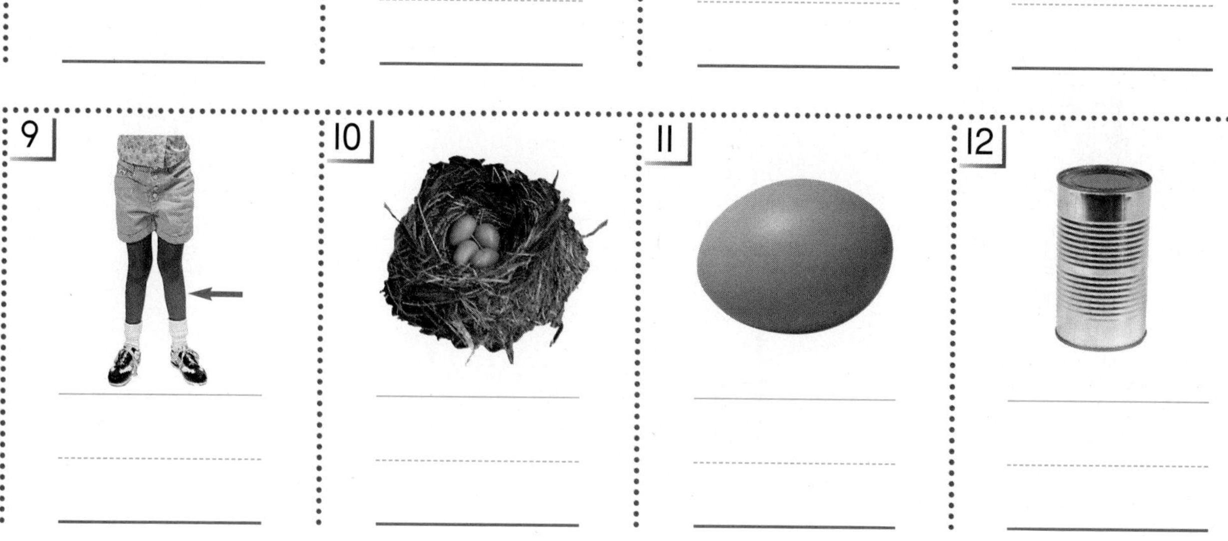

Say each picture name.
Write e if you hear the short e sound.
Color each short e picture.

 Name ______________________________

Say the word that names the first picture. Circle the pictures whose names rhyme with the word.

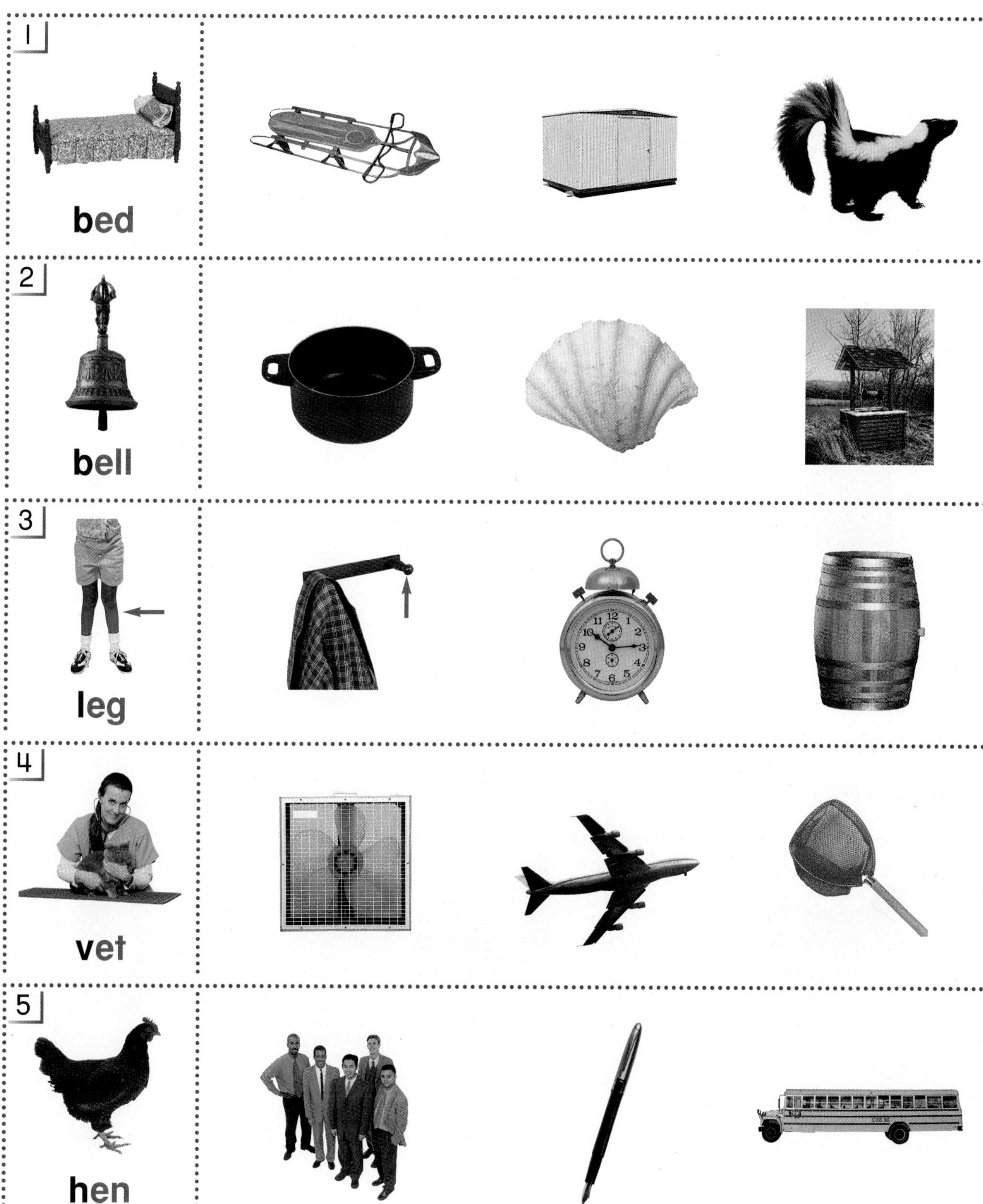

Say each picture name. Trace the first letter.
Then write ell to make the word.

1 b

2 y

3 t

4 w

5 f

Say each picture name. Trace the first letter.
Then write en to make the word.

6 h

7 m

8 t

 Name ______

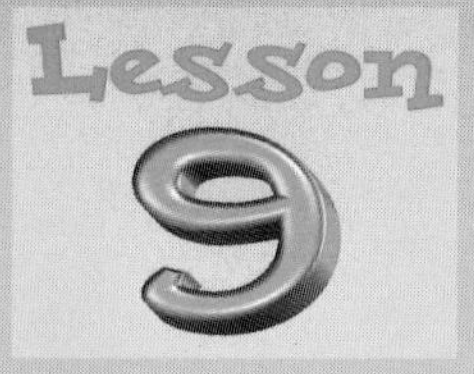

Lesson 9 Short i

I i

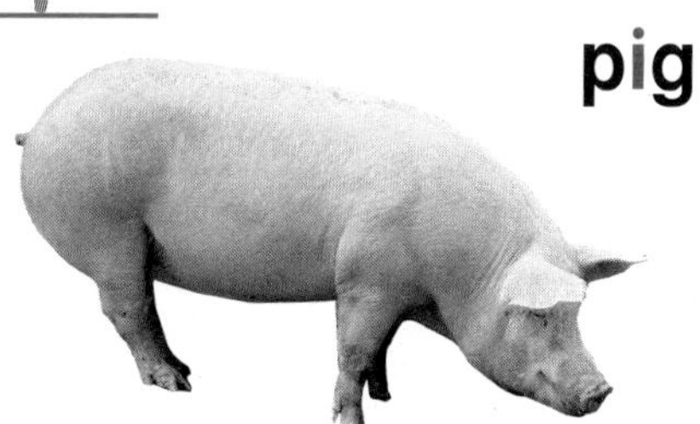

pig

Pig has the short i sound.
Say each picture name.
Write i if you hear the short i sound.

1
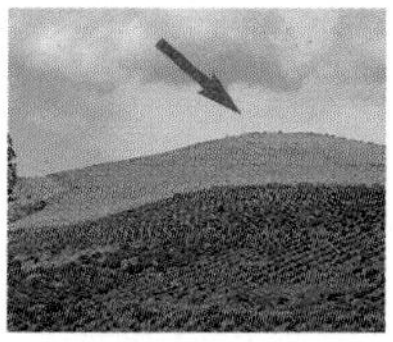
i

2
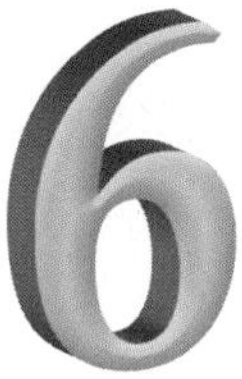

3
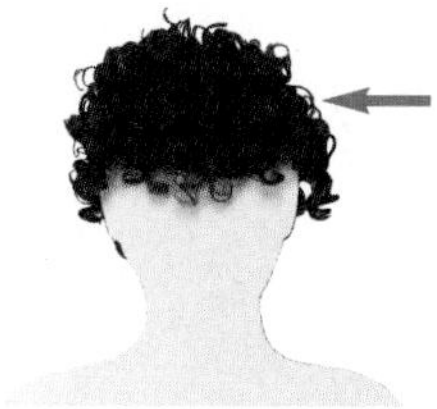

4
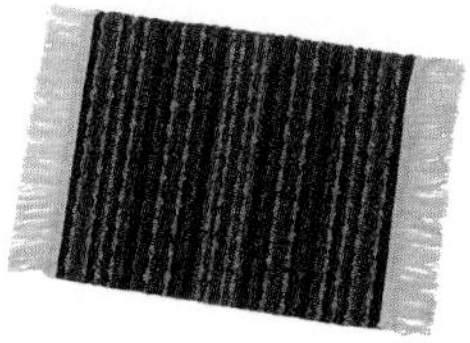

5
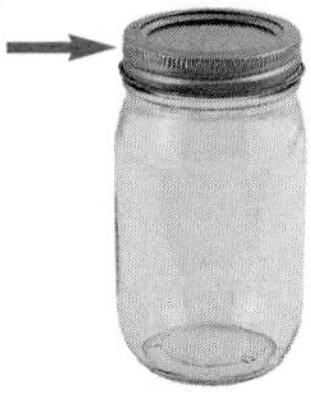

6
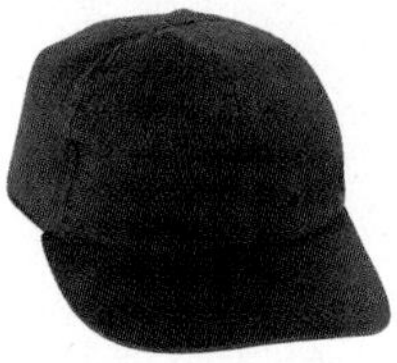

7
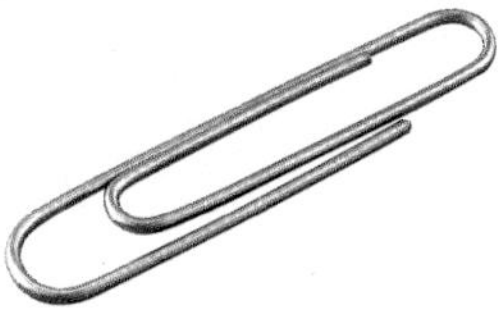

8
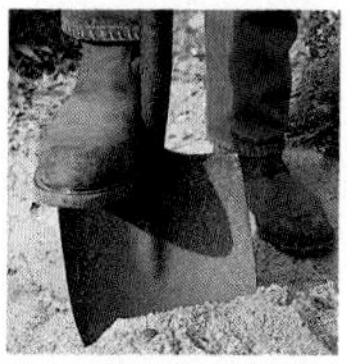

9
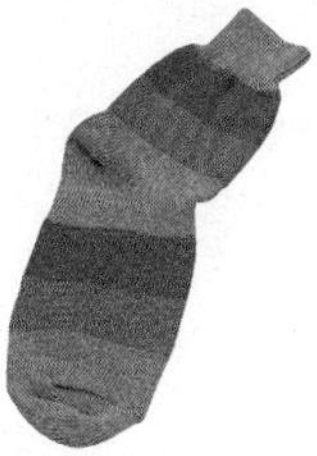

10
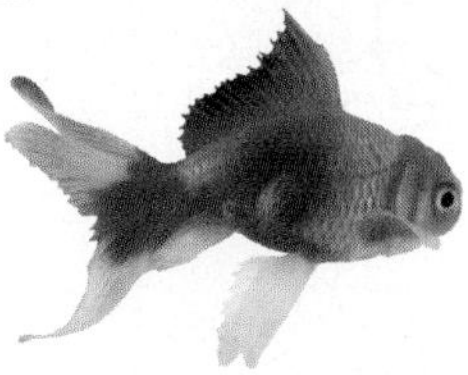

11
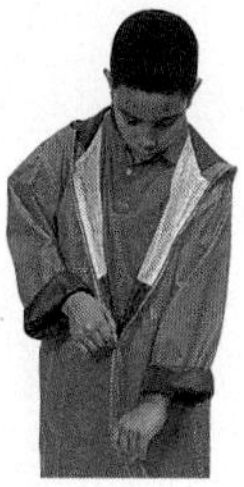

12
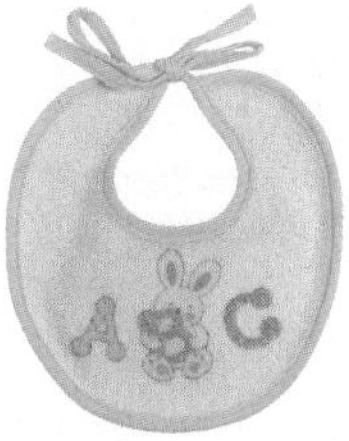

Say each picture name.
Write i if you hear the short i sound.
Color each short i picture.

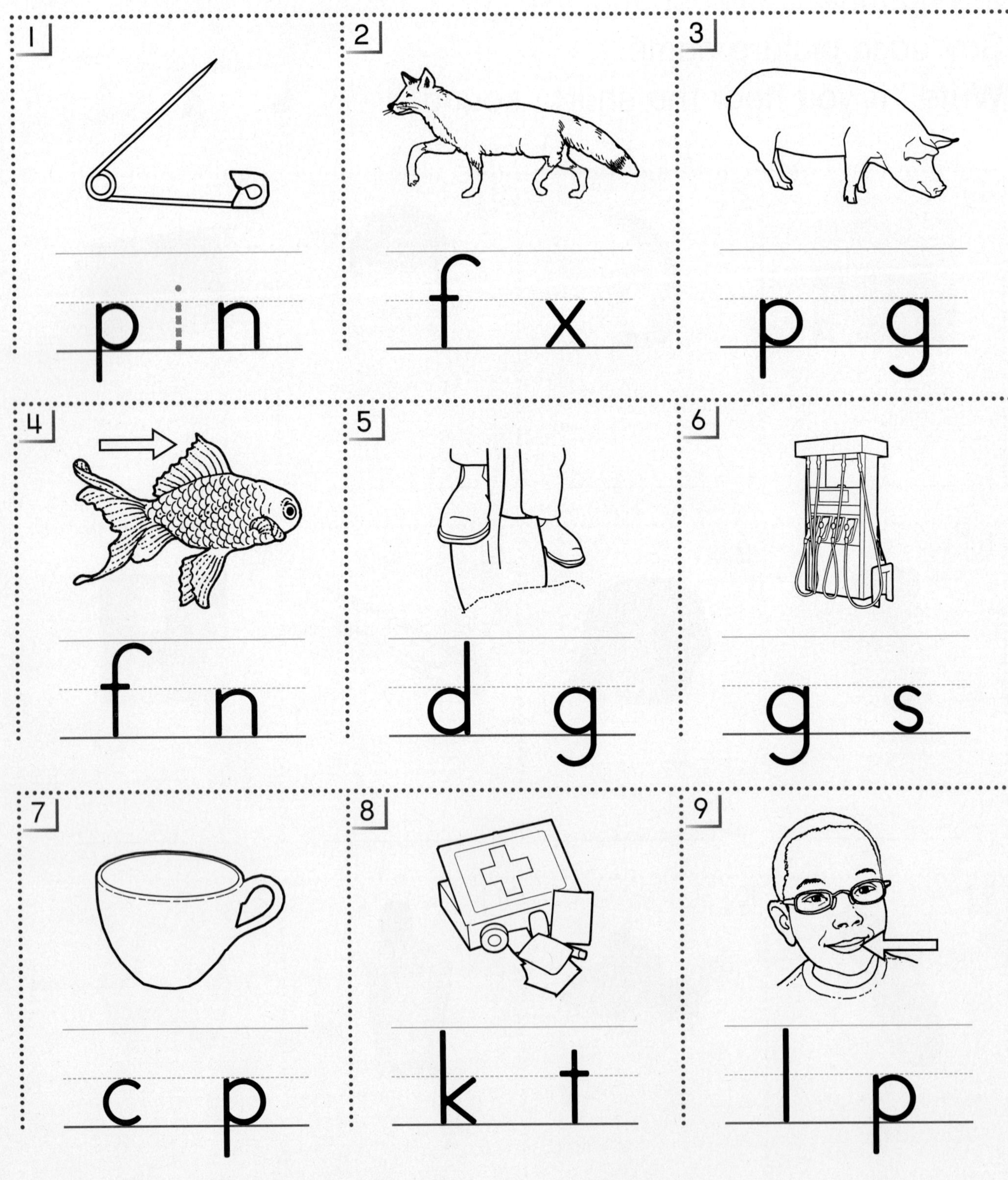

Say the word that names the first picture. Circle the pictures whose names rhyme with the word.

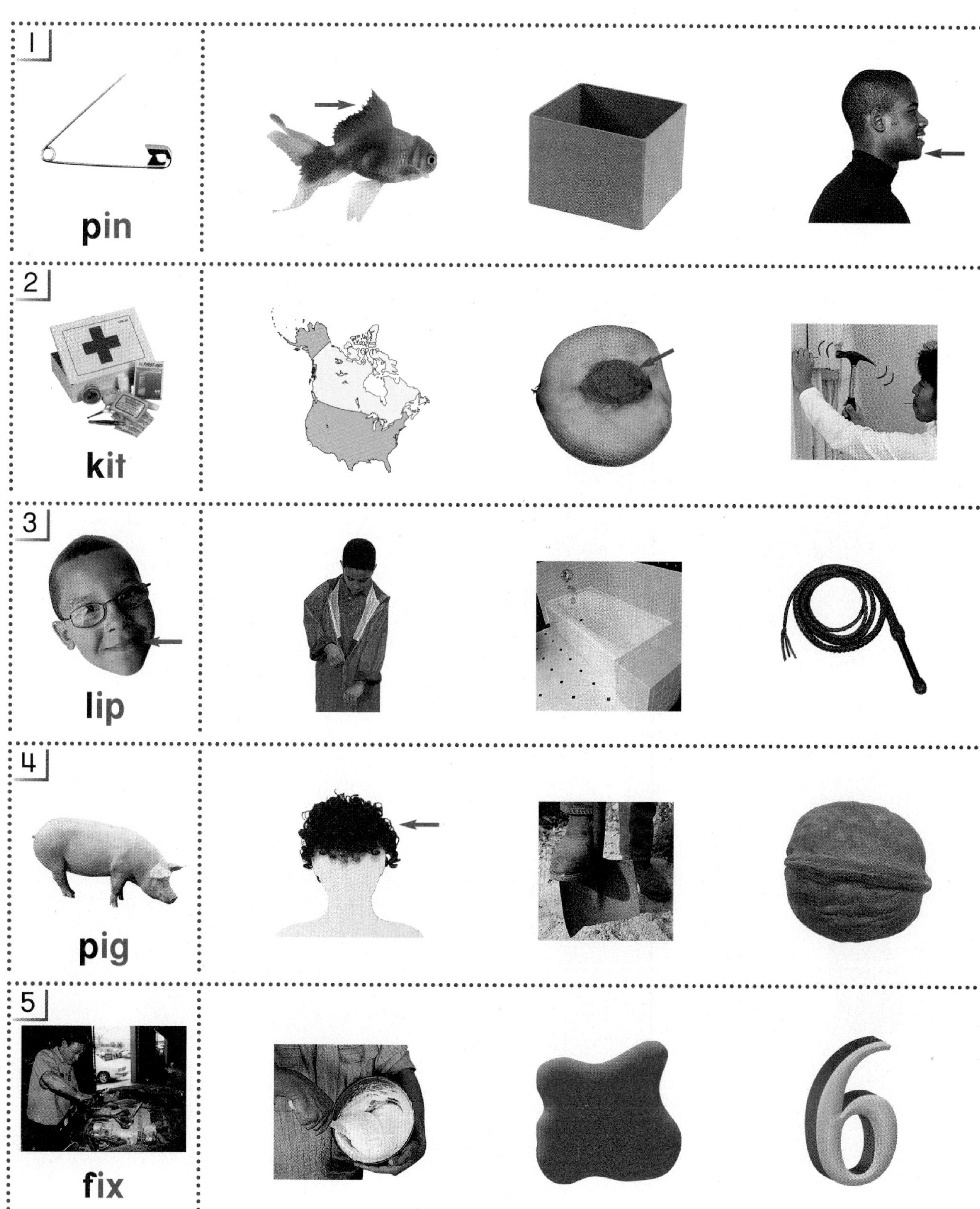

Say each picture name. Trace the first letter.
Then write it to make the word.

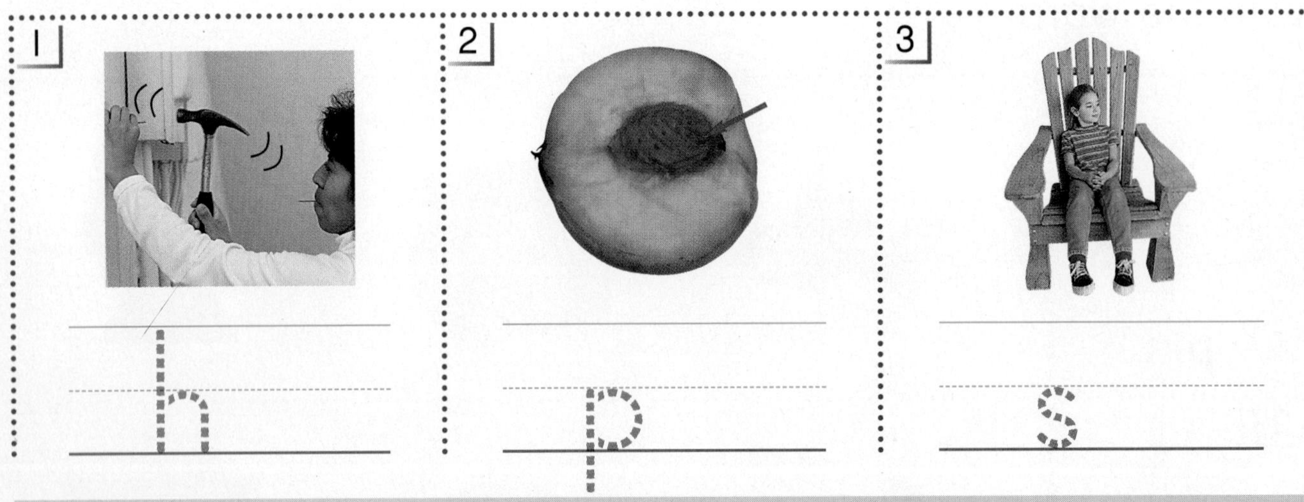

1 h

2 p

3 s

Say each picture name. Trace the first letter.
Then write ig to make the word.

4 d

5 p

6 w

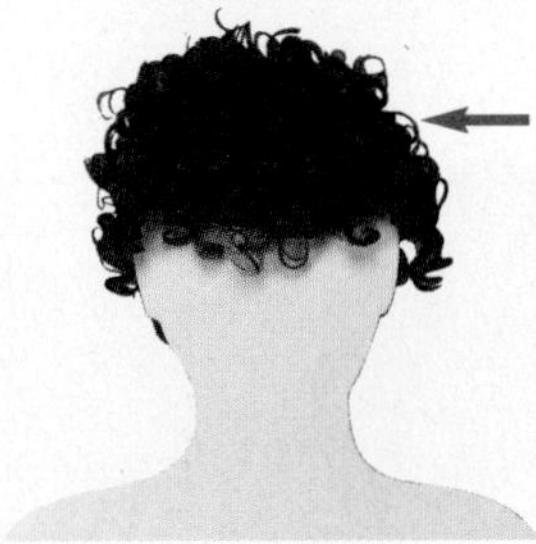

7 b

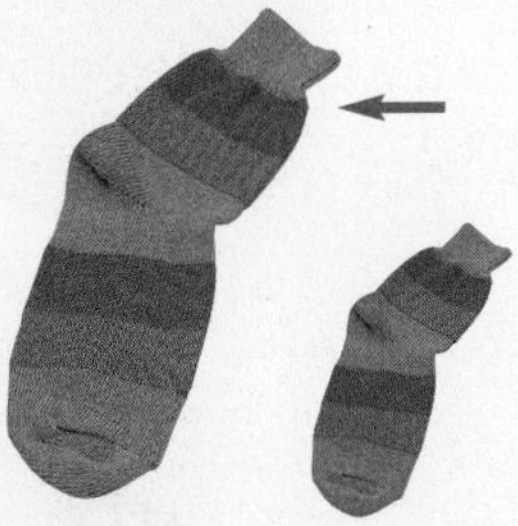

 Name ____________________

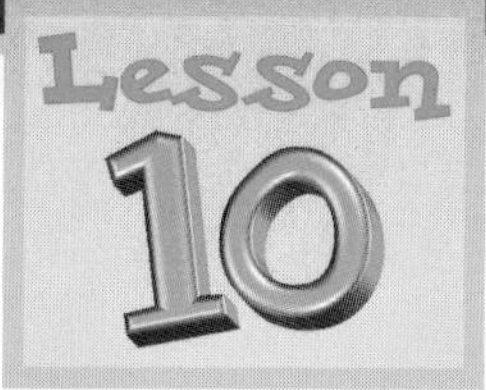

Lesson 10

Short o

O o

pop

Pop has the short o sound.
Say each picture name.
Write o if you hear the short o sound.

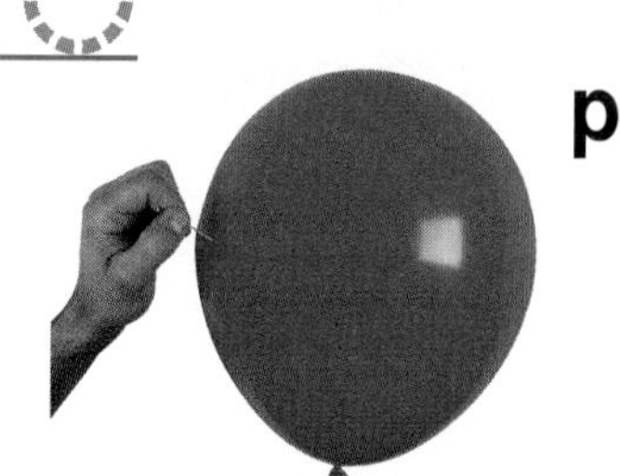

1

o

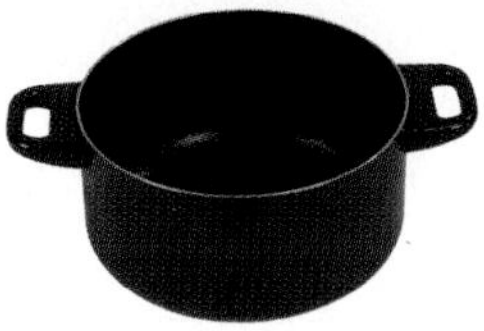

2

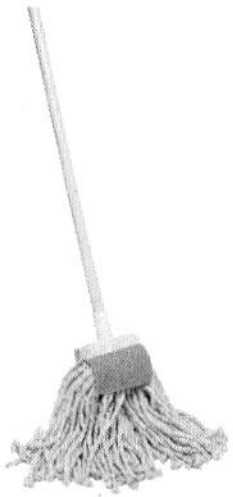

3

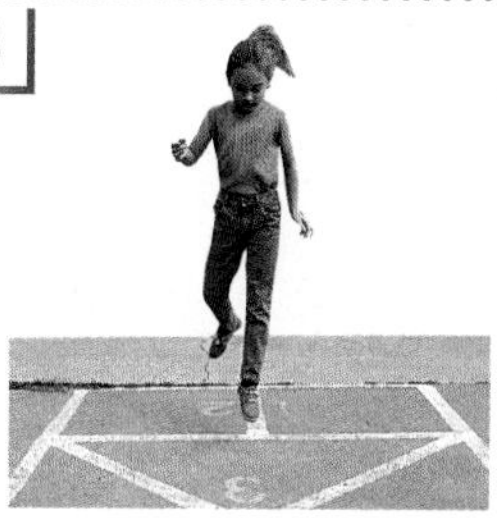

4

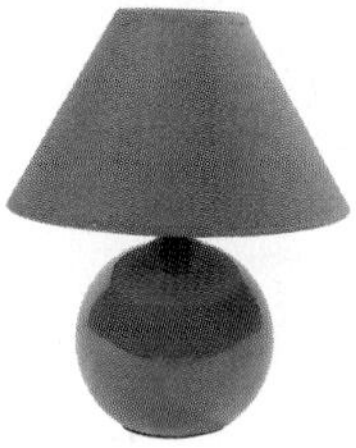

5

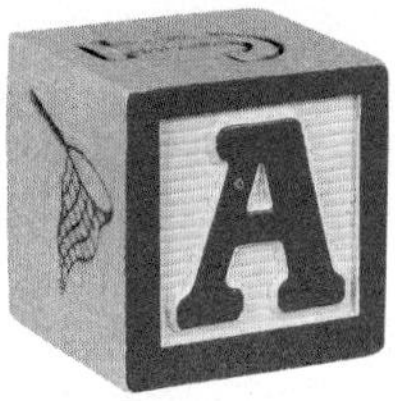

6

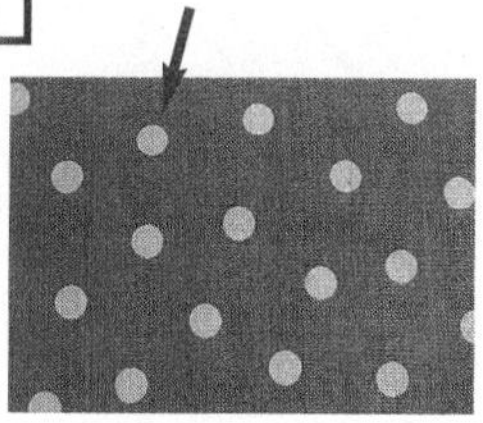

7

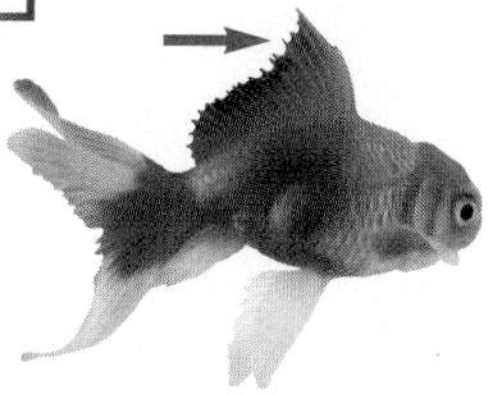

8

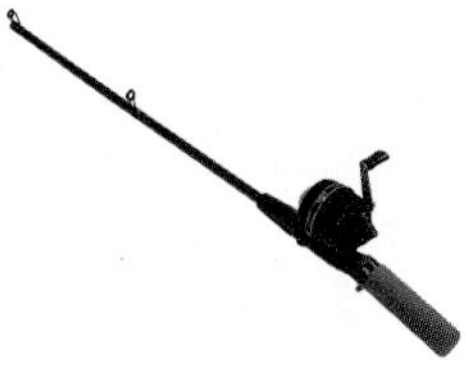

9

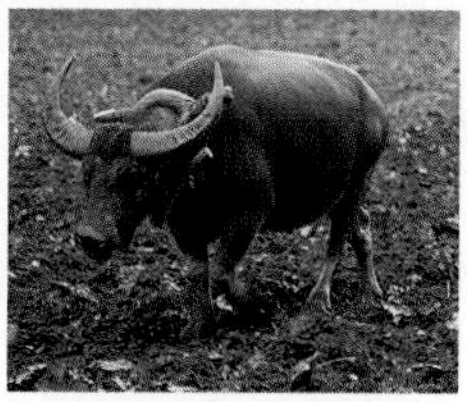

10

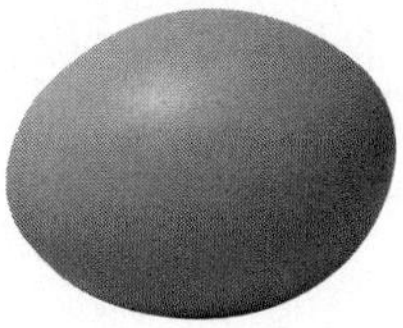

11

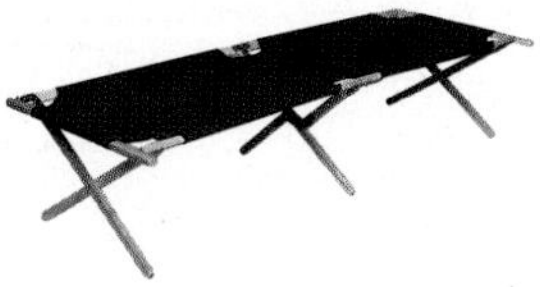

12

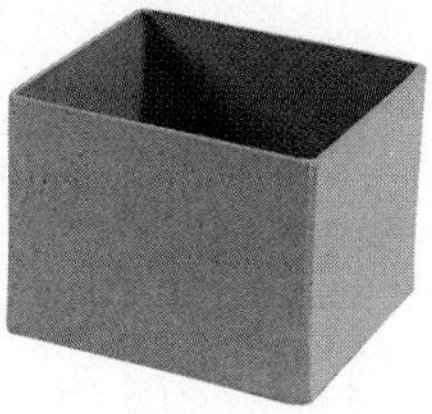

Say each picture name.
Write o if you hear the short o sound.
Color each short o picture.

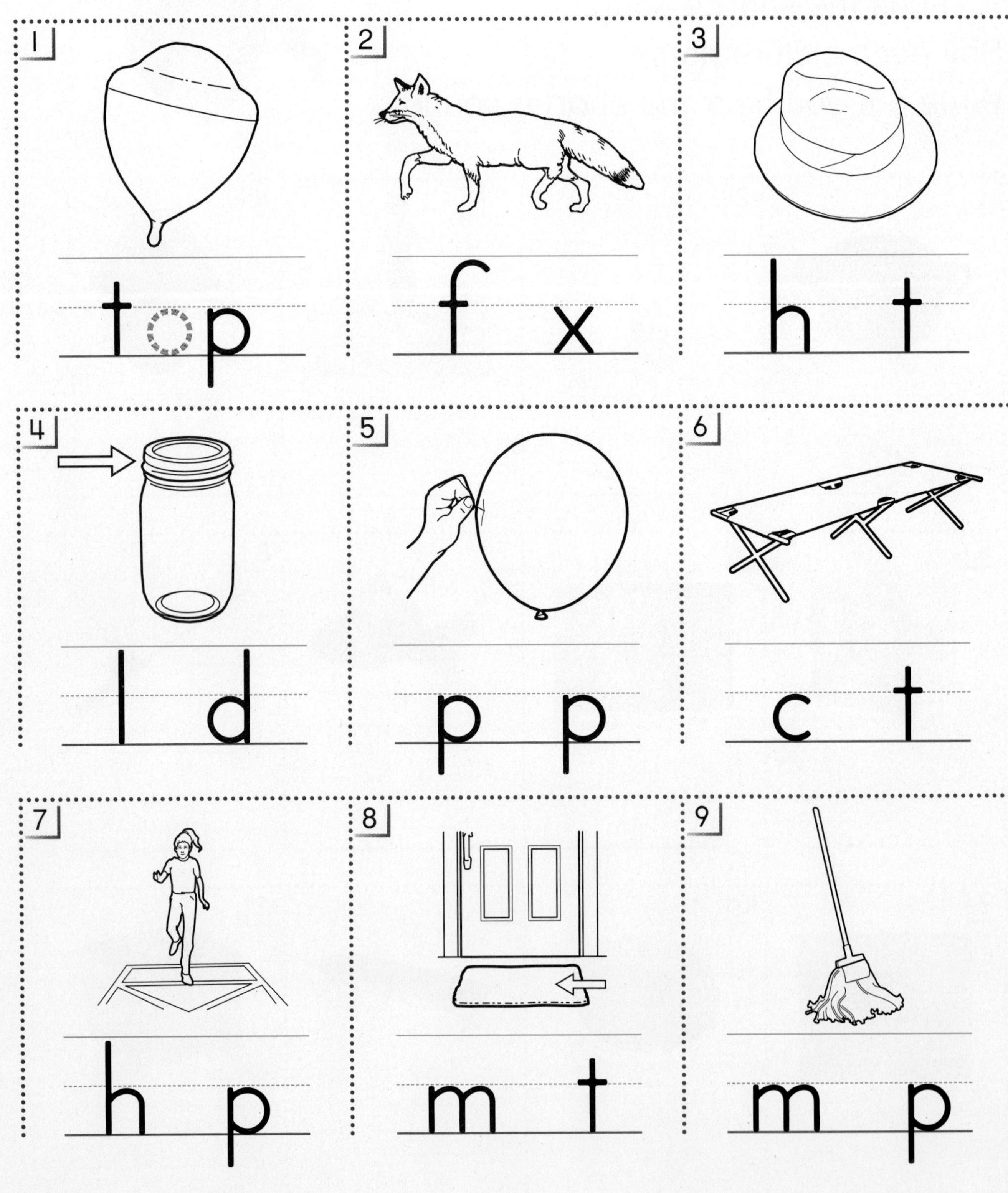

 Name ______________________________

Say the word that names the first picture. Circle the pictures whose names rhyme with the word.

Say each picture name. Trace the first letter.
Then write op to make the word.

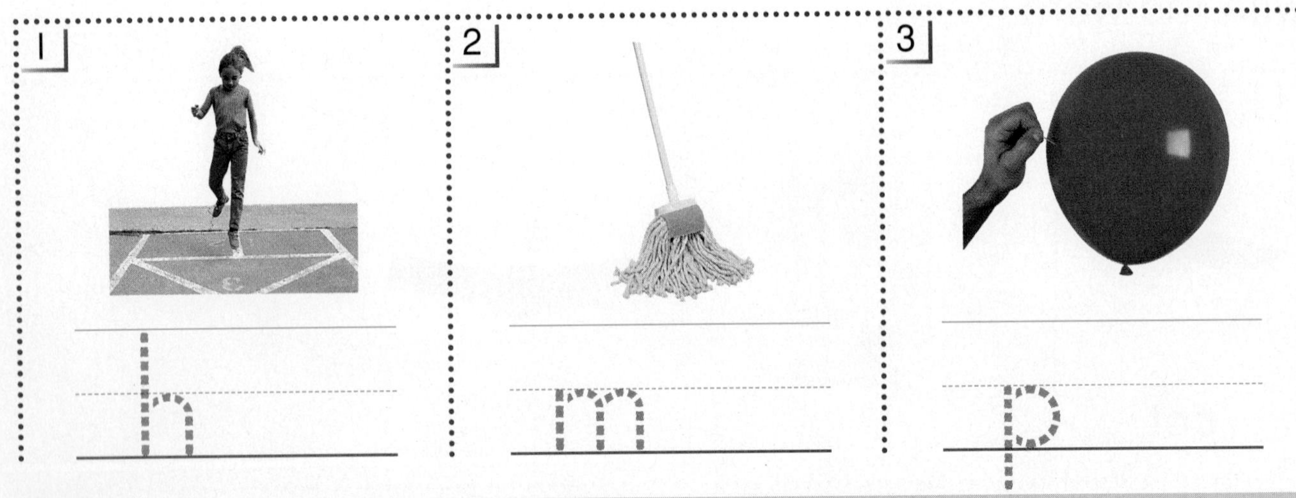

1

h

2

m

3

p

Say each picture name. Trace the first letter.
Then write ot to make the word.

4

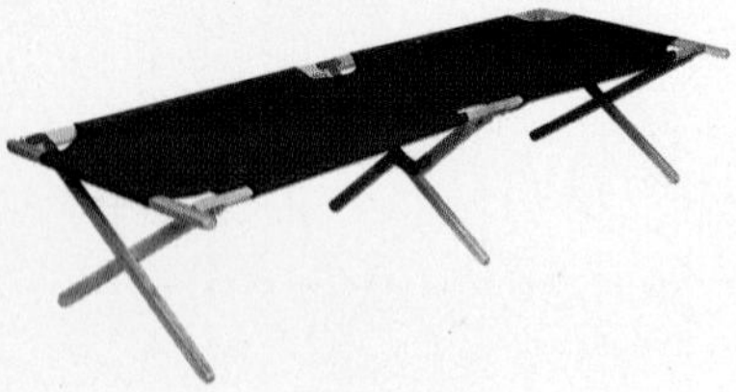

c

5

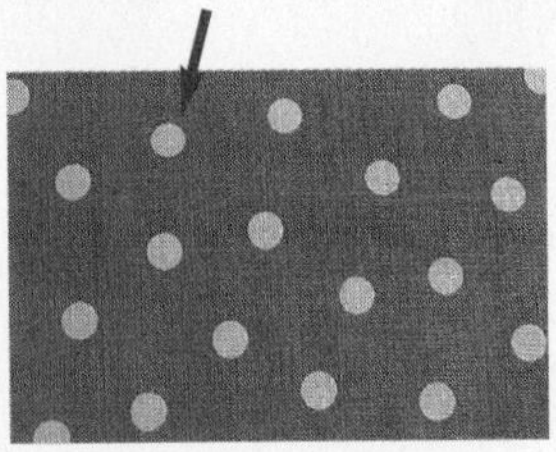

d

6

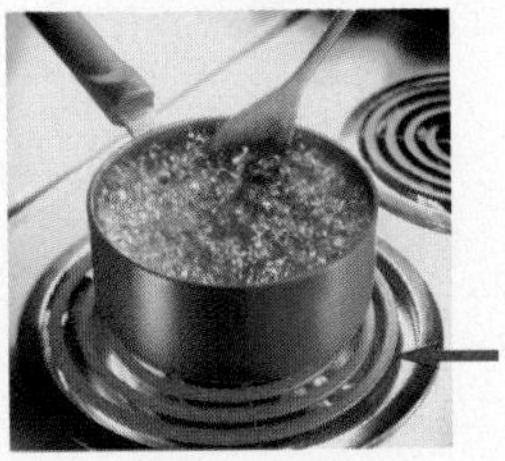

h

7

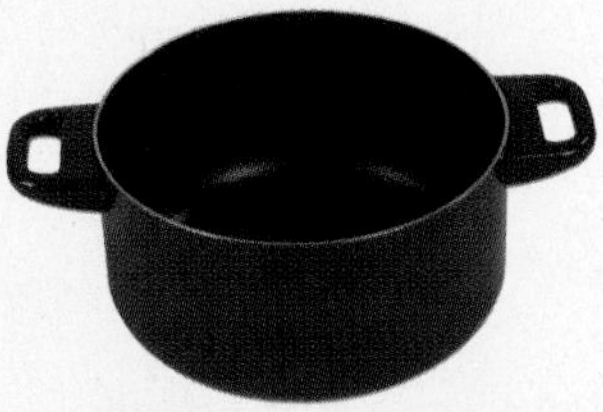

p

Name

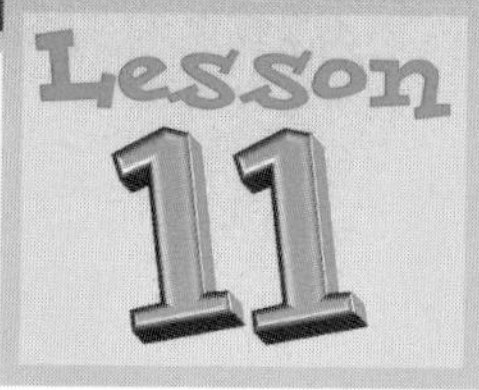

Lesson 11

Short u

Uu

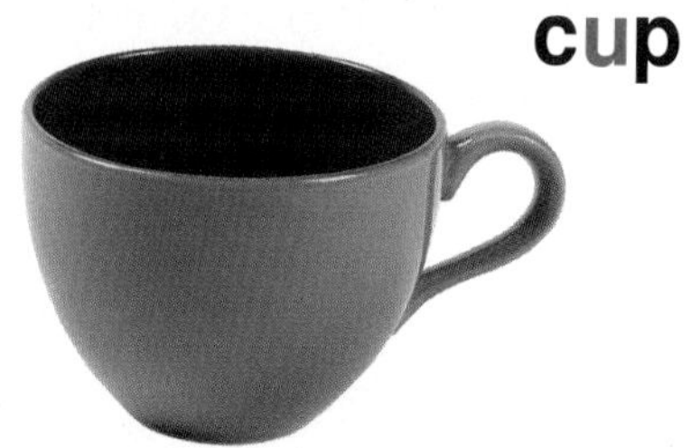

Cup has the short u sound.
Say each picture name.
Write u if you hear the short u sound.

cup

1

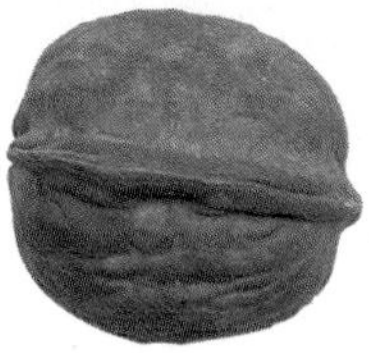

u

2

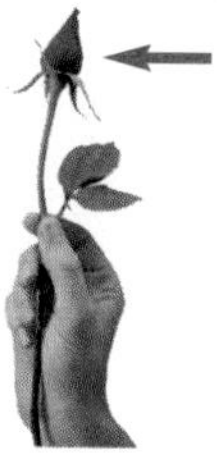

3

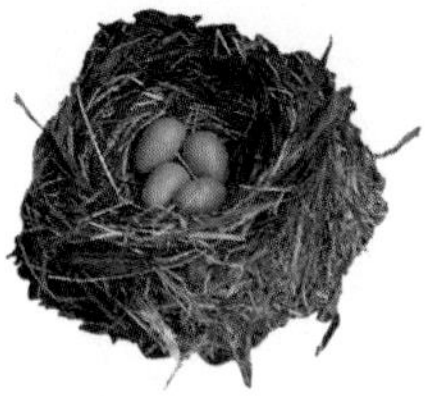

4

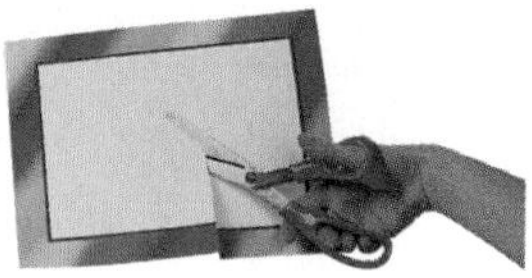

5

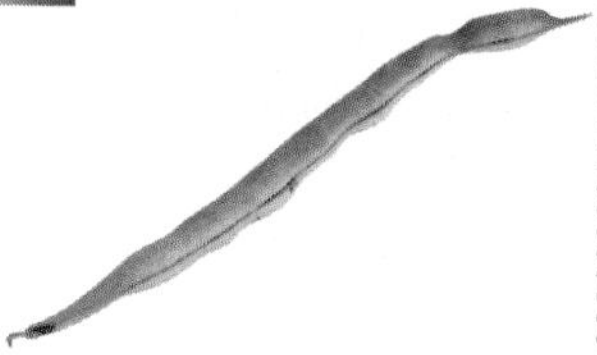

6

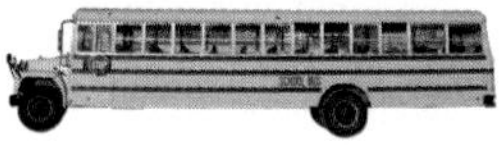

7

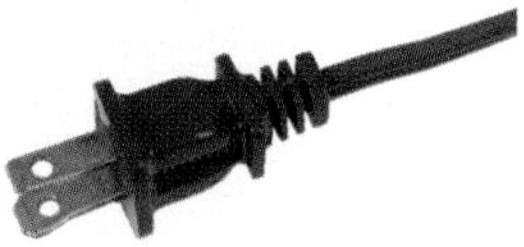

8

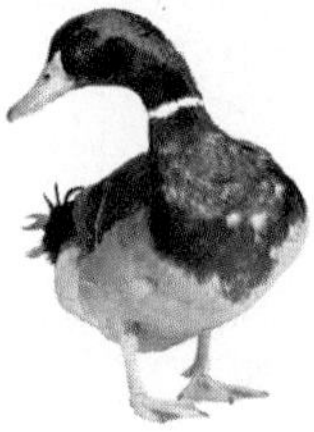

9

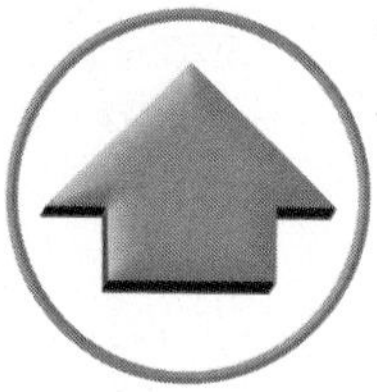

10

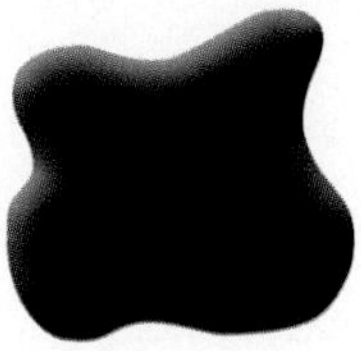

11

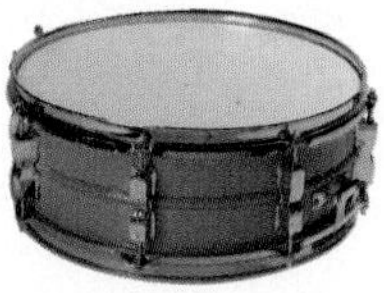

12

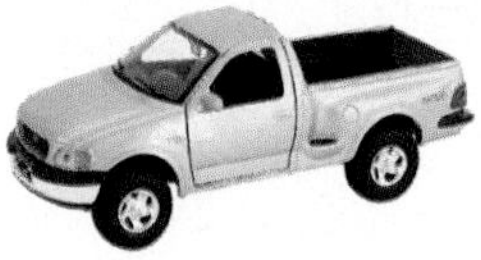

Say each picture name.
Write u if you hear the short u sound.
Color each short u picture.

 Name ______________________________

Say the word that names the first picture.
Circle the pictures whose names rhyme with the word.

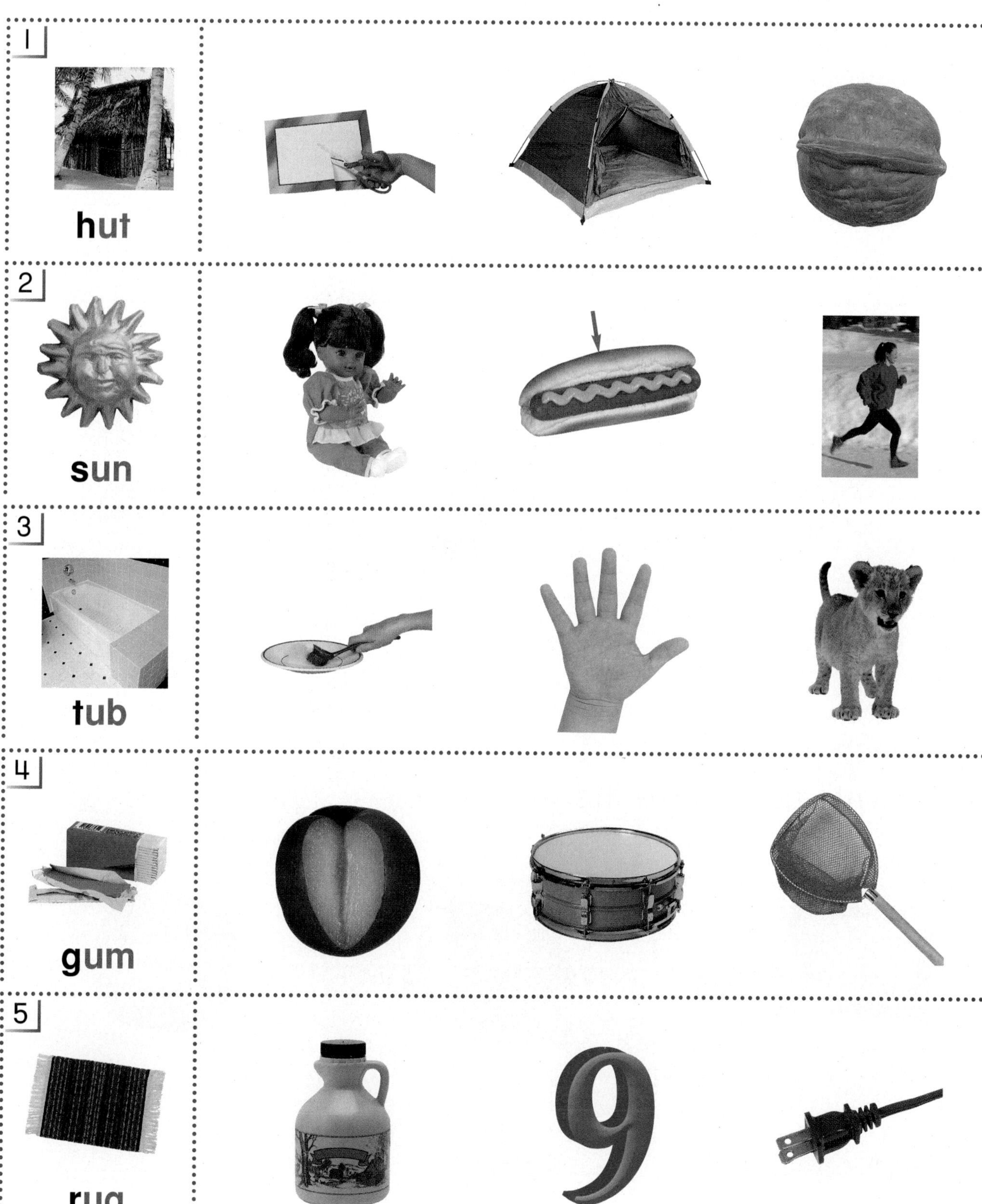

Say each picture name. Trace the first letter.
Then write ug to make the word.

1
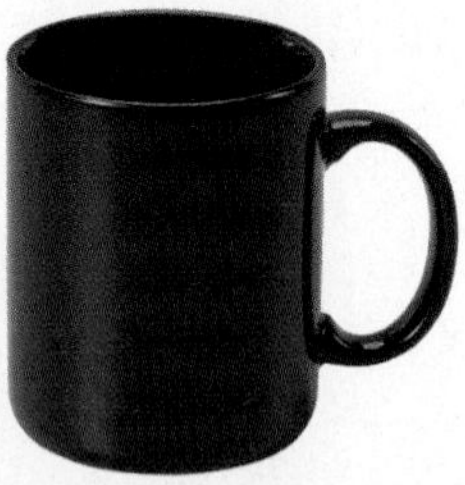
m

2
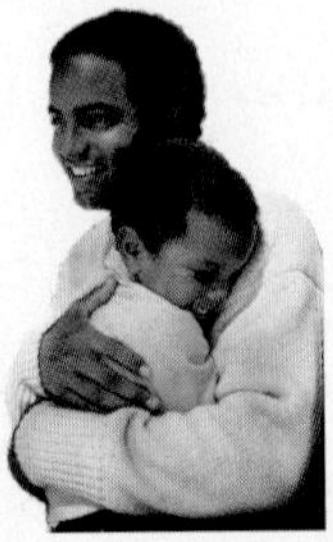
h

3
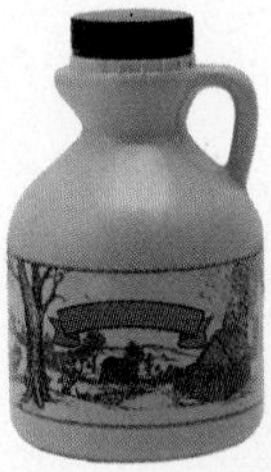
j

4
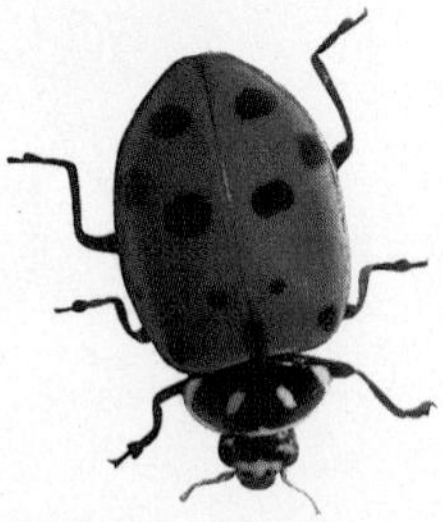
b

5
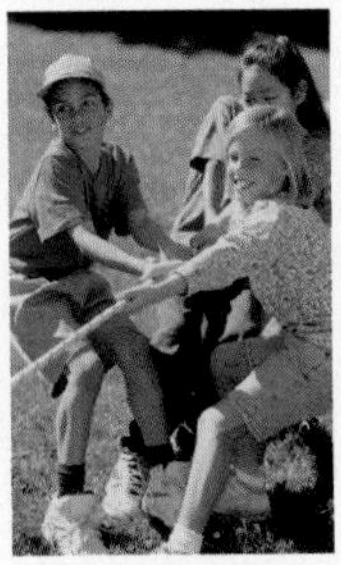
t

6
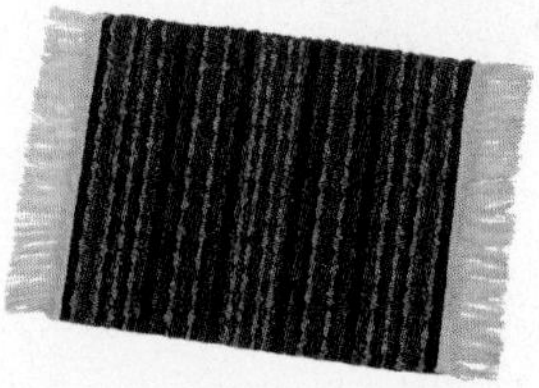
r

Say each picture name. Trace the first letter.
Then write ut to make the word.

7
c

8
h

9
n

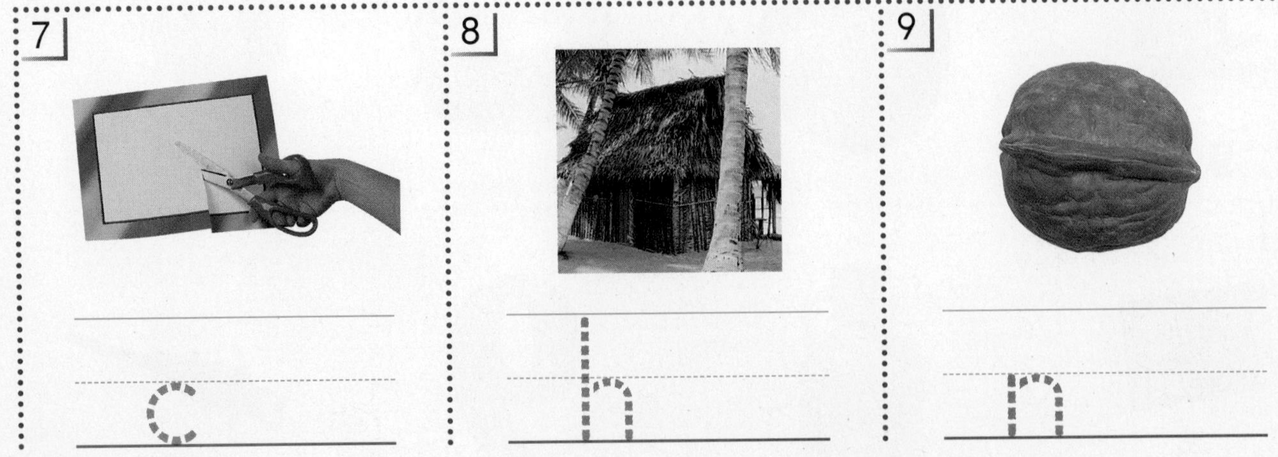

 Name ________________

Unit 2 Review Lessons 7–11

Say each picture name. Circle the letter for the vowel sound. Then write the letter.

cat  bed  pig 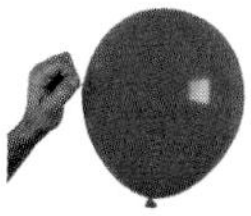 pop  cup

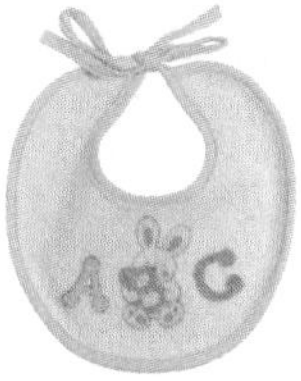

1	2	3
u e o	a i u	e u o
nut	b b	r d

4	5	6
o e u	i a u	e u o
w b	m p	v st

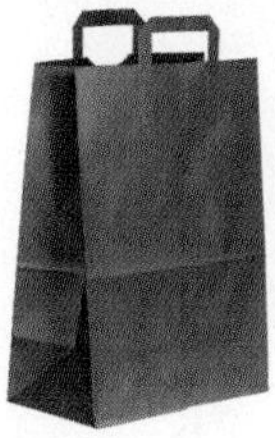

7	8	9
i a o	e u o	a u o
z p	d ck	b g

Say each picture name.
Write the letter for the vowel sound.

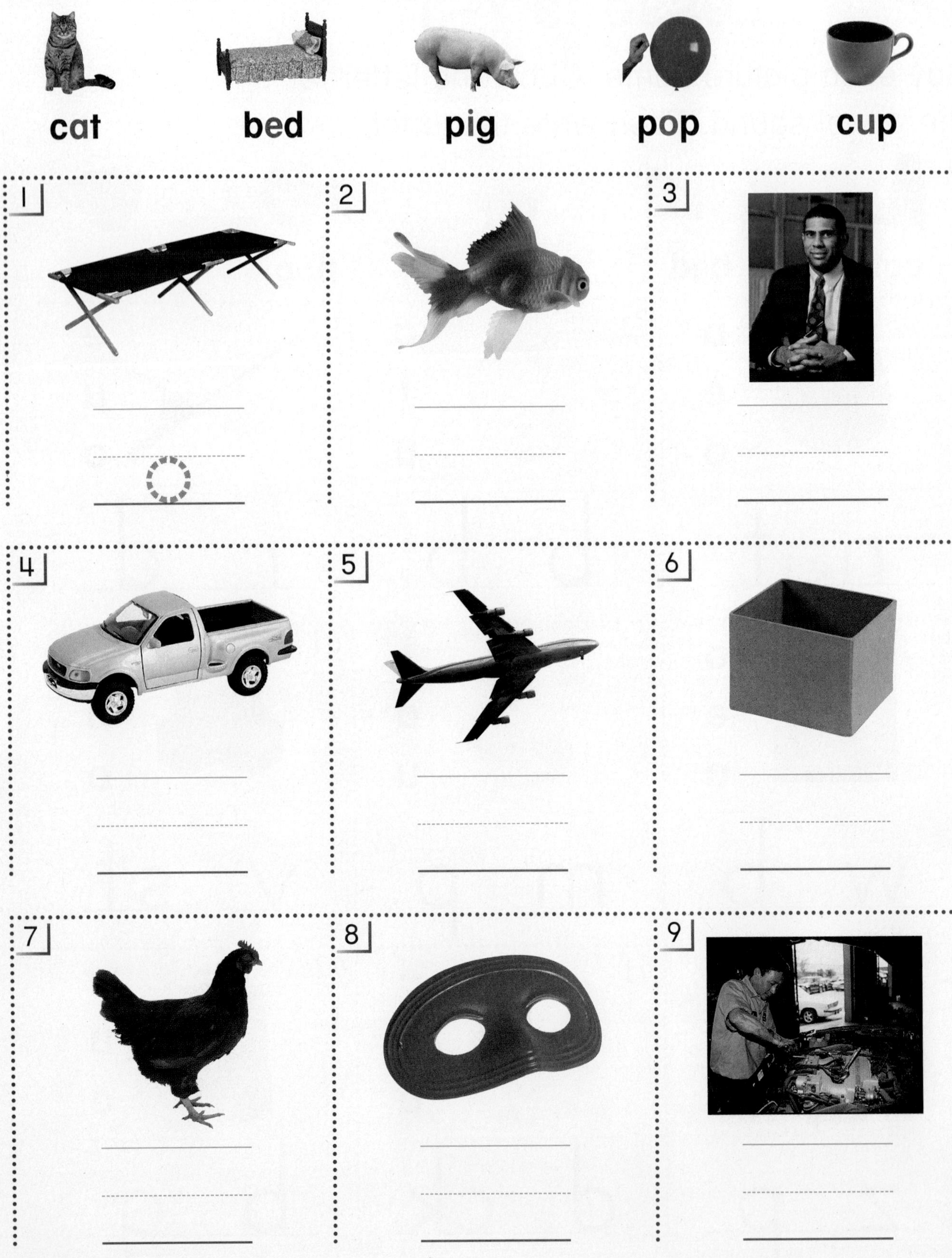

 Name ____________________

Say the word that names the first picture. Circle the pictures whose names rhyme with the word.

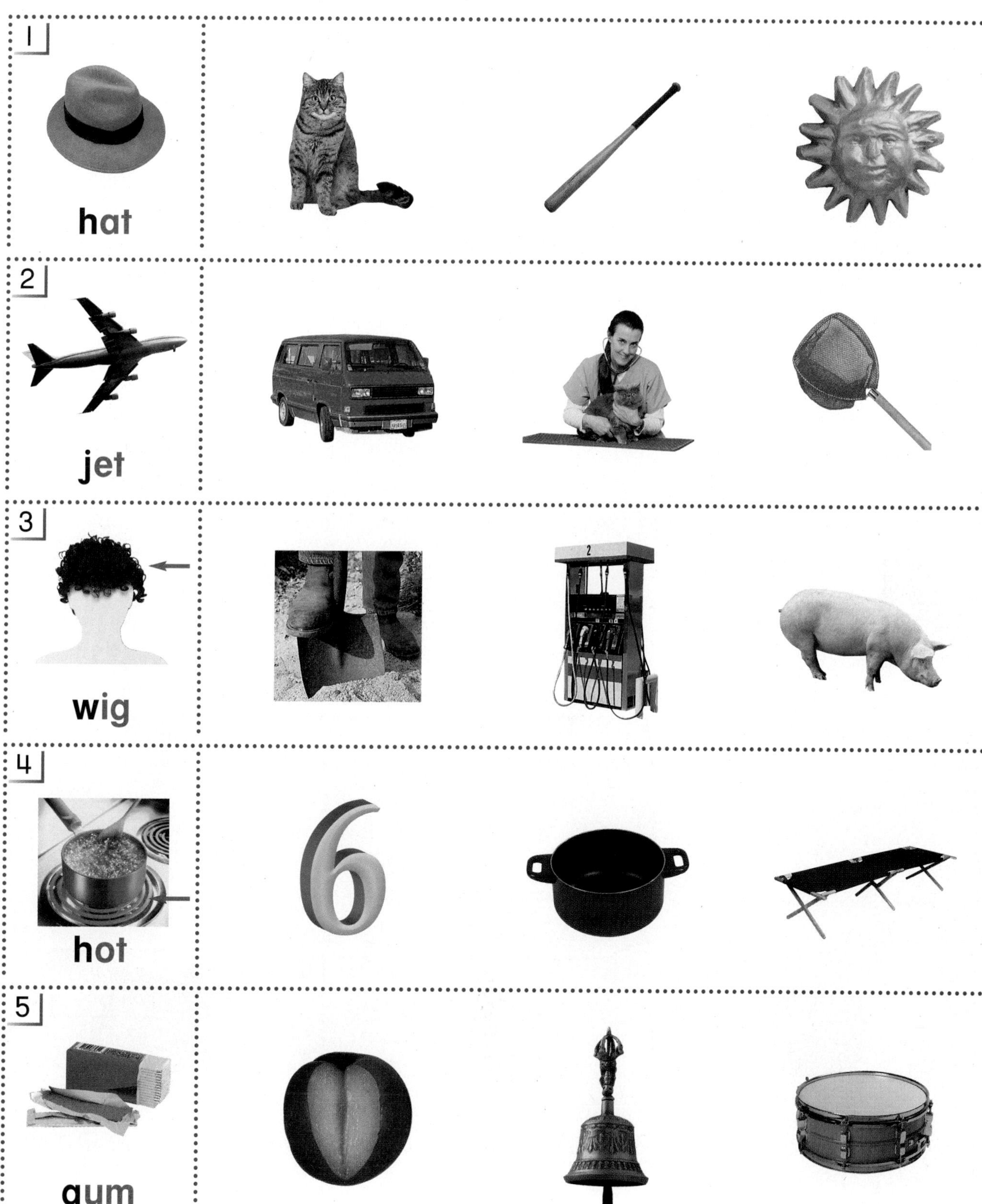

Say each picture name. Trace the first letter.
Then write the letters from the box that complete the name.

an	en	in	op	ut

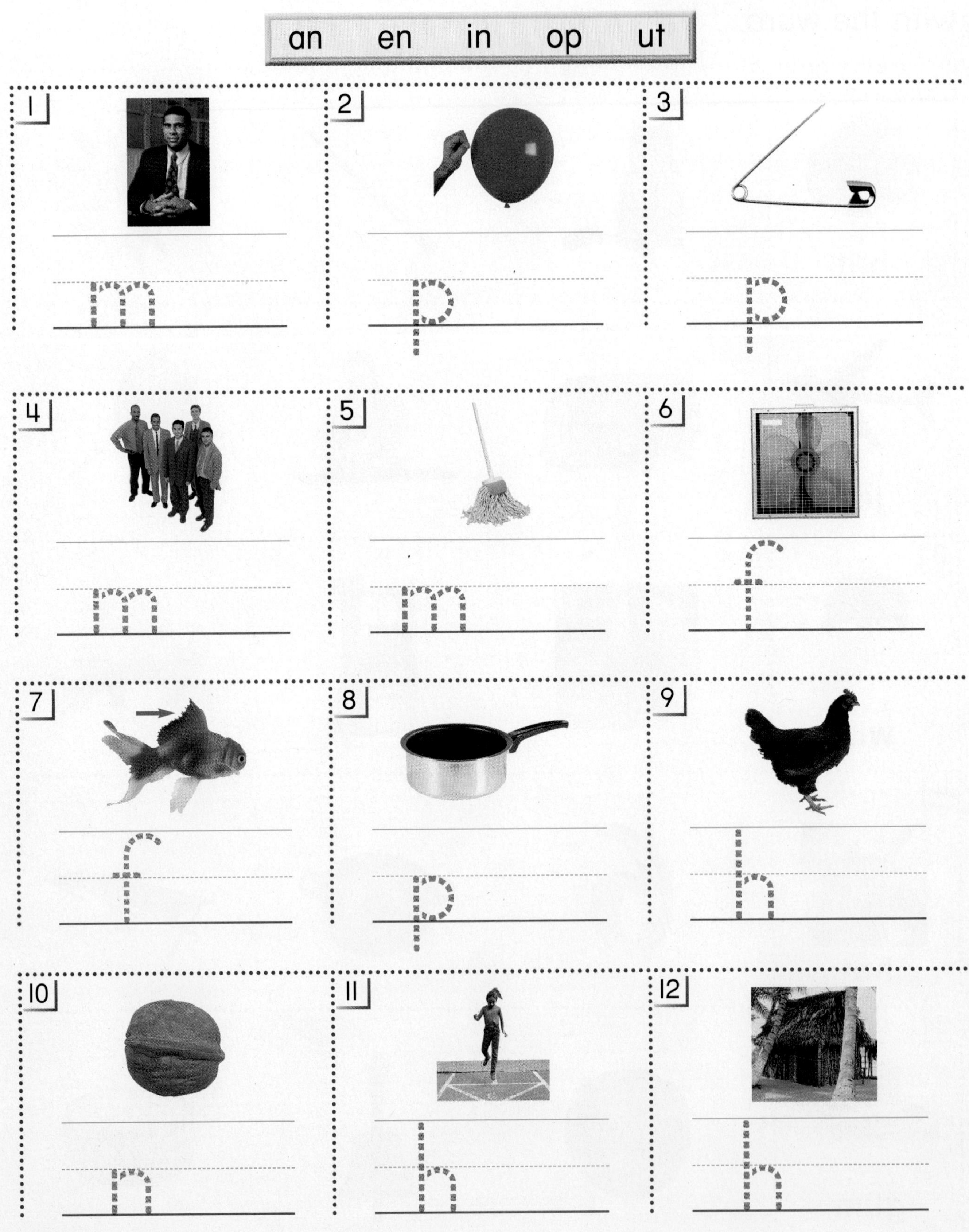

 Name ______________________________

Words with Short a

Say and Write

1. am
2. at
3. can
4. ran

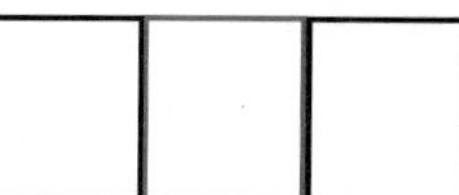

5. fast

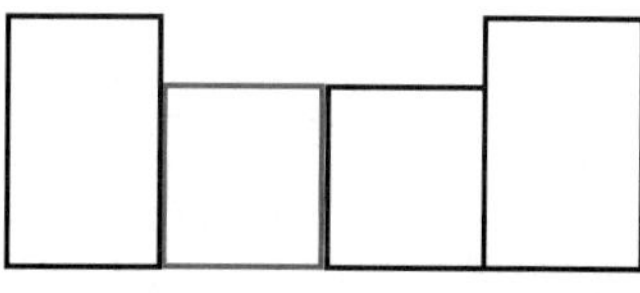

6. last

The short a sound can be spelled a.

ran

fast

Spell and Write

Write the spelling word that completes each sentence.

1. I ______________ Pam.

2. A duck ______________ swim.

3. The dog is ______________ the park.

4. The pig ______________ to him.

5. My dog can run ______________.

6. The frog is ______________.

 Name ______________________________

Read and Write

Write the spelling words to complete the story.

- am
- at
- can
- ran
- fast
- last

Randy Rabbit ________________ on a path. The path was ________________ the park. Randy ran well. He ran ________________. That was ________________ week.

Now he will run again. "I ________________ ready," Randy says. "I ________________ do it!"

Proofreading

Circle each word that is spelled wrong.
Write the word correctly.

Dad,

Lunch is et 11:00.

We cin meet then.

I im in Room 102.

Sam

1. ______

2. ______

3. ______

Language Skills

A sentence that tells something ends with a period.

Lad is my dog.

Write each sentence correctly.

4. Lad is fast

______

5. We ran to Dad

______

6. I was the last one

______

 Name ______

More Words with Short a

Say and Write

1. sat
2. van
3. has
4. hand
5. that
6. have

The short a sound can be spelled a.

van

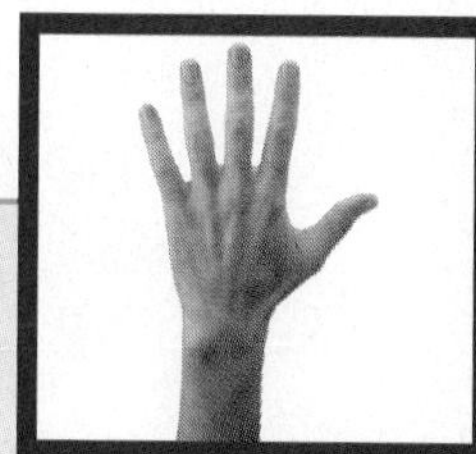
hand

sat	hand
van	that
has	have

Spell and Write

Write the spelling word that completes each sentence.

1. Mack has a ____________.

2. Will you get ____________ for me?

3. Dan can draw his ____________.

4. Jan ____________ by her pal.

5. Hal and Jack ____________ big bags.

6. My cat ____________ a bell.

Name ____________________________

Read and Write

Write the spelling words to complete the selection.

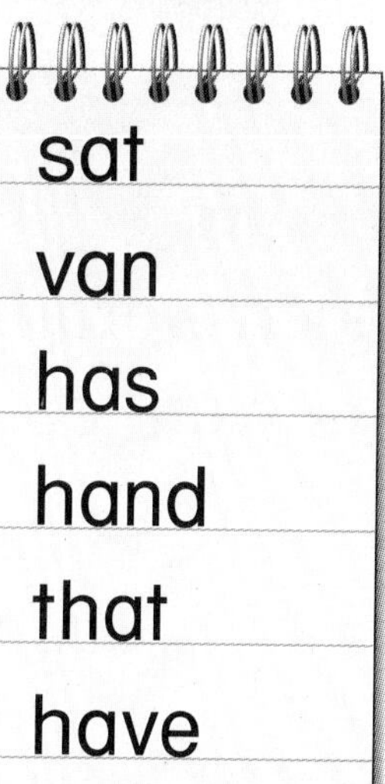

Nan __________ with her dad. Nan had a book in her __________. She got it from Books on Wheels. Books on Wheels is a __________. It __________ many good books in it. Nan likes __________ van. Do you __________ Books on Wheels where you live?

Proofreading

Circle each word that is spelled wrong.
Write the word correctly.

Jack's List

1. Help wash the vaan.
2. Find out who hes my cap.
3. Get that book for Gran.

1. ____________

2. ____________

3. ____________

Language Skills

A sentence begins with a capital letter.

Stan has a van.

Write each sentence correctly.

4. we have a van.

5. i sat in back.

6. mom held my hand.

 Name ____________

Lesson 15 Words with Short e

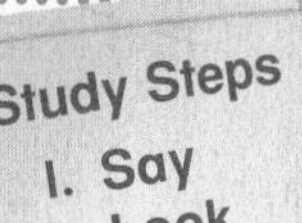
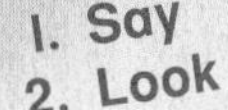

Study Steps
1. Say
2. Look
3. Spell
4. Write
5. Check

Say and Write

1. end
2. ten
3. red
4. wet
5. tell
6. seven

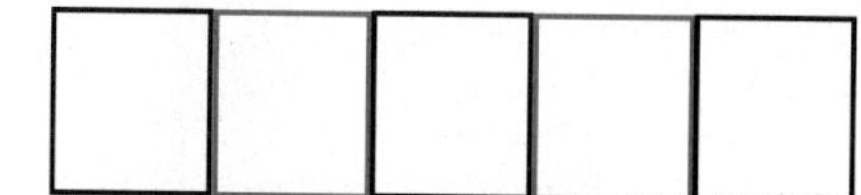

The short e sound can be spelled e.

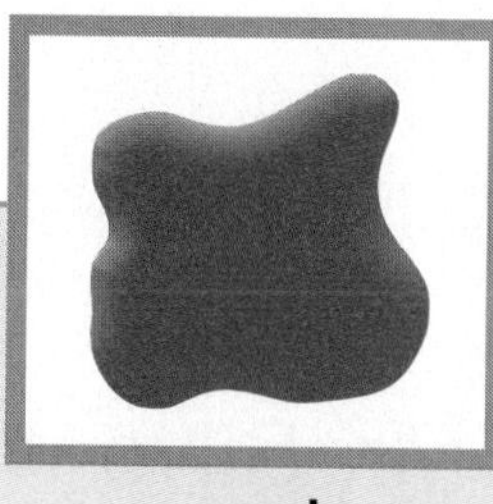
red

tell

end	tell
ten	seven
red	
wet	

Spell and Write

Write the spelling word that completes each sentence.

1. The dog is ________.

2. Ben's hat is ________.

3. Five plus five is ________.

4. I am at the ________ of the line.

5. Three plus four is ________.

6. Mr. Silva will ________ a story.

 Name ________________

Read and Write

Write the spelling words to complete the story.

end
ten
red
wet
tell
seven

Rex washes his socks. Some are ________.

Some are white. The socks are dripping ________.

Rex puts them on the line. He has five pairs. There are

________ socks on the line. Three socks on the

________ fall. Now only ________ socks

are on the line. Who will ________ Rex?

Proofreading

Circle each word that is spelled wrong. Write the word correctly.

There were tun pets in bed.

Then sevin fell out.

How does this story ind?

1. ______

2. ______

3. ______

Dictionary Skills

Look at the Spelling Dictionary. The words are in ABC order. Words that begin with a come first.

4. Write the first word in the Spelling Dictionary.

______

5. Write the last word in the Spelling Dictionary.

______

6. Write a Spelling Dictionary word that begins with c.

______

7. Write a Spelling Dictionary word that begins with m.

______

 Name ______

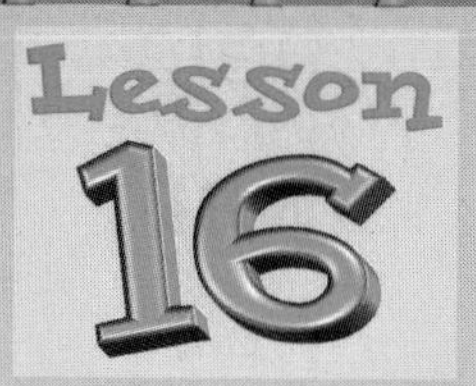

Lesson 16 More Words with Short e

Say and Write

1. get

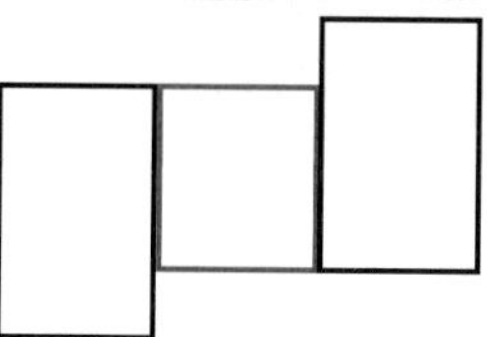

2. pet

3. help

4. went

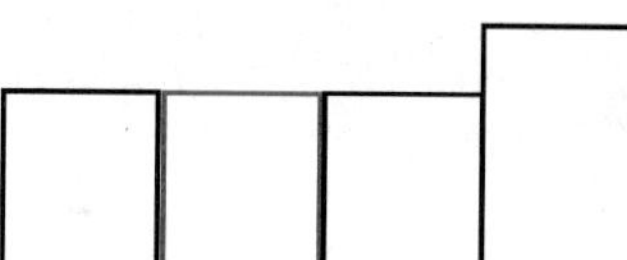

5. best

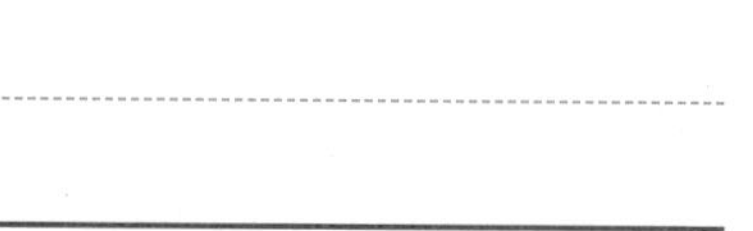

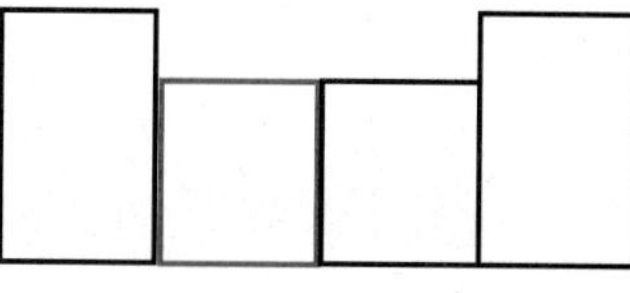

6. when

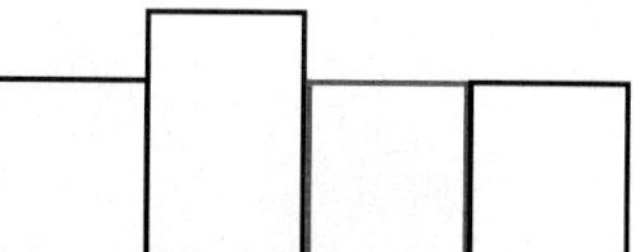

The short e sound can be spelled e.

pet

help

Spell and Write

Write the spelling word that completes each sentence.

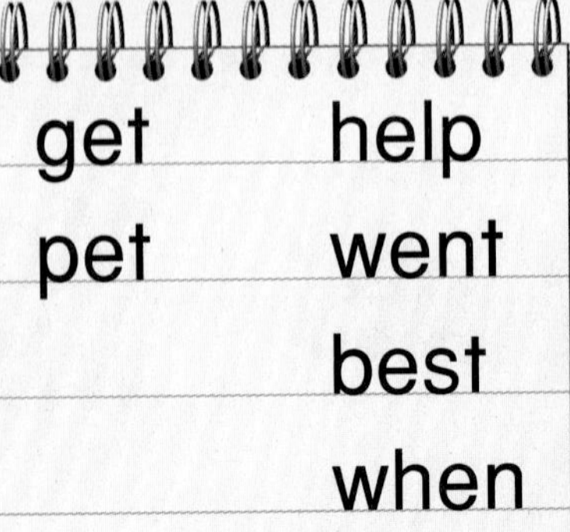

1. Brett's ______________ is a dog.

2. My cat naps ______________ I nap.

3. This dog is the ______________!

4. Dad ______________ to the store.

5. Ted and Ned ______________ the plants.

6. Ken can ______________ his mom.

 Name ______________

Read and Write

Write the spelling words to complete the selection.

get
pet
help
went
best
when

A puppy is a good ________. Would you like to ________ a puppy? You can ________ take care of it. You can feed your puppy ________ it is hungry. You can play with it. You will wonder where the time ________. Do you think a puppy is the ________ pet?

Proofreading

Circle each word that is spelled wrong.
Write the word correctly.

Help Wanted

I need help with my pett.

You must feed it whin I am gone.

I need the bist.

1. ______________________

2. ______________________

3. ______________________

Writing

Write a sentence about a pet. Use a spelling word.

____

____

Name ______________________________

Lesson 17 Words with Short i

Say and Write

1. in
2. is
3. it
4. with

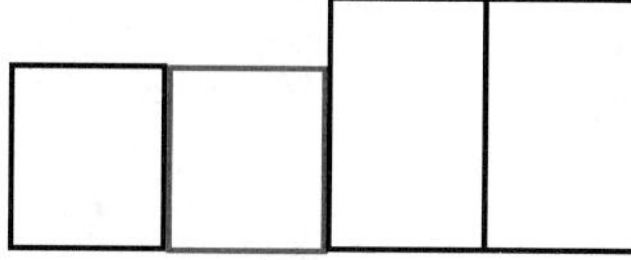

5. sick

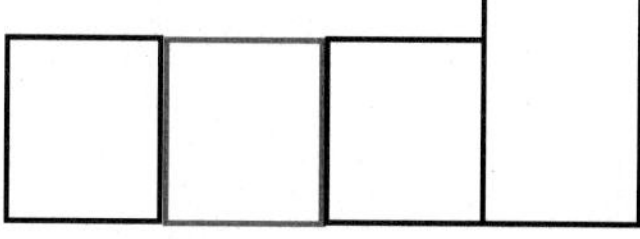

6. quit

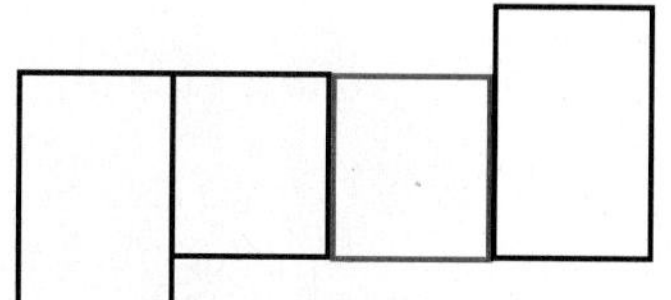

The short i sound can be spelled i.

in

sick

in	with
is	sick
it	quit

Spell and Write

Write the spelling word that completes each sentence.

1. Nick feels ______________.

2. I have milk ______________ my fish.

3. He ______________ happy.

4. Kim plays ______________ the yard.

5. Jim wants the rain to ______________.

6. The flower has a bee on ______________.

Name ______________________________

Read and Write

Write the spelling words to complete the selection.

- in
- is
- it
- with
- sick
- quit

Sometimes people get ________. Then they must stay ________ bed. It ________ not much fun. You can make a picture for a sick friend. Get some paper. Draw on ________. Paint on it ________ bright colors. Don't ________ until it looks great. Give it to your friend. Say, "Get well quick!"

Proofreading

Circle each word that is spelled wrong.
Write the word correctly.

Will,

Are you seck?

Hot tea iz good.

Stay en bed and rest.

Jim

1. ____________________

2. ____________________

3. ____________________

Dictionary Skills

Write the spelling words in ABC order.

quit   with   it   sick

4. ____________________   5. ____________________

6. ____________________   7. ____________________

Name ____________________

Unit 3 Review
Lessons 13–17

Word Math

Add letters and take away letters.
Write the spelling word.

am	can	fast

1. ham – h = __________

2. fan – n + st = __________

3. cap – p + n = __________

Proofreading

Circle the word that is spelled wrong. Write it correctly.

has	that	have

4. Dad and I hav hats. __________

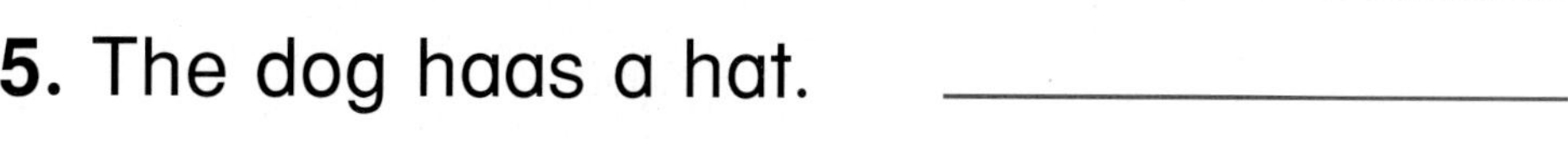

5. The dog haas a hat. __________

6. Is thet my hat? __________

Proofreading

seven end tell

Help Hen find her nest.

Draw the path that has correctly spelled words.

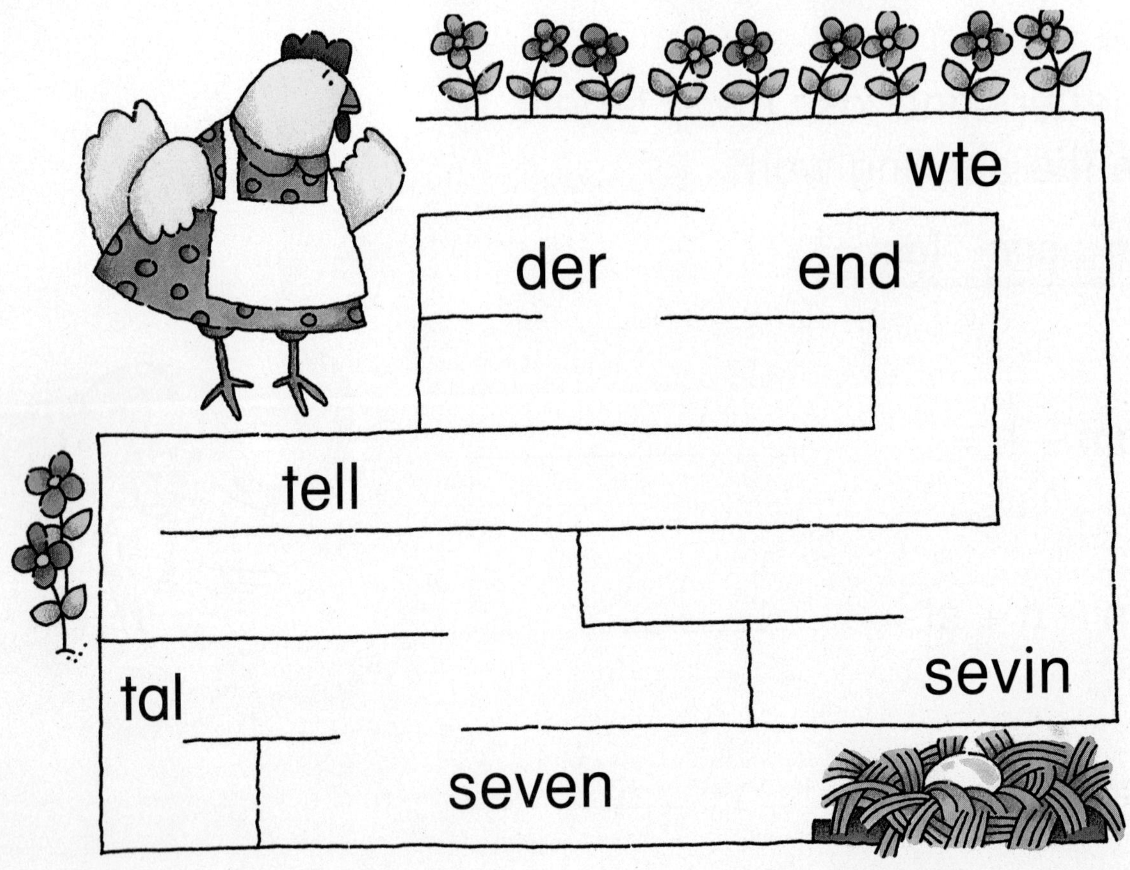

Dictionary Skills

Look at the path above.

Write the correctly spelled words in ABC order.

1. ______________________

2. ______________________

3. ______________________

Name ______________________

Missing Words

Write the word that completes each sentence.

get help when

1. Ben will ____________ a puppy.

2. Beth likes to ____________ Dad cook.

3. We will go ____________ it gets dark.

What's the Right Word?

The word in dark type does not make sense in the sentence. Write the spelling word that makes sense.

in sick with

4. Rex is white **quit** brown spots. ____________

5. Do you feel **pig**? ____________

6. The cans are **it** the bag. ____________

Write About It

Jenny likes to swim. She can swim fast.
What do you like to do? Write about it.
The words in the box may help you.

am	get
can	seven
fast	when
have	in
that	is
end	with

Name ______________________

More Words with Short i

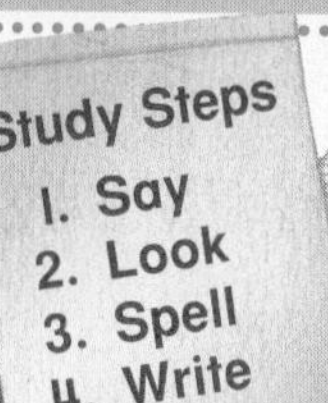

Say and Write

1. if
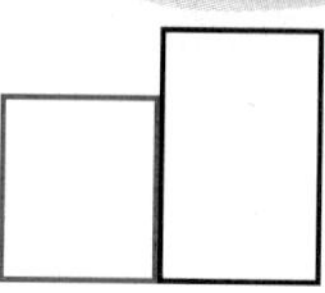
2. six
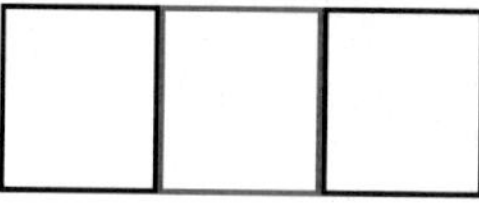
3. sit
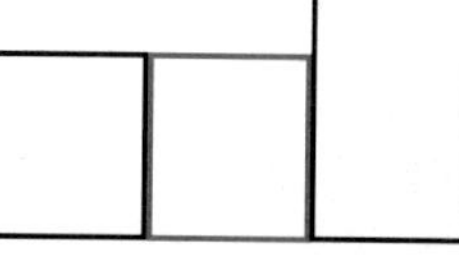
4. big
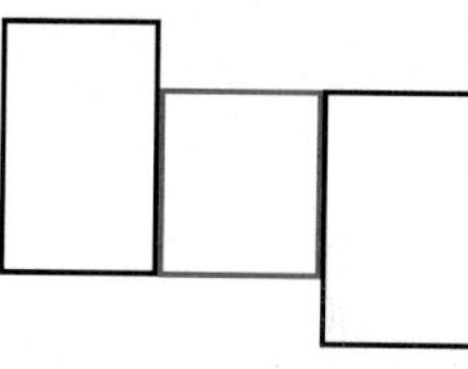
5. did
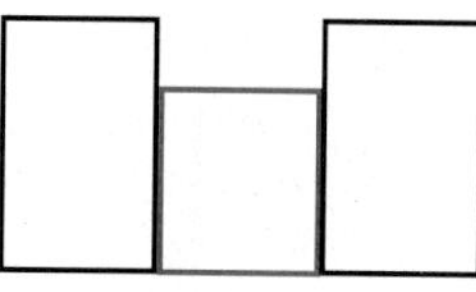
6. this

The short i sound can be spelled i.

six

big

if	big
six	did
sit	this

Spell and Write

Write the spelling word that completes each sentence.

1. Milly has ______________ puppies.

2. We will get wet ______________ it rains.

3. We ______________ together.

4. The red box is the ______________ one.

5. Dad and I ______________ the shopping.

6. I drew ______________.

 Name ______________________________

Read and Write

Write the spelling words to complete the story.

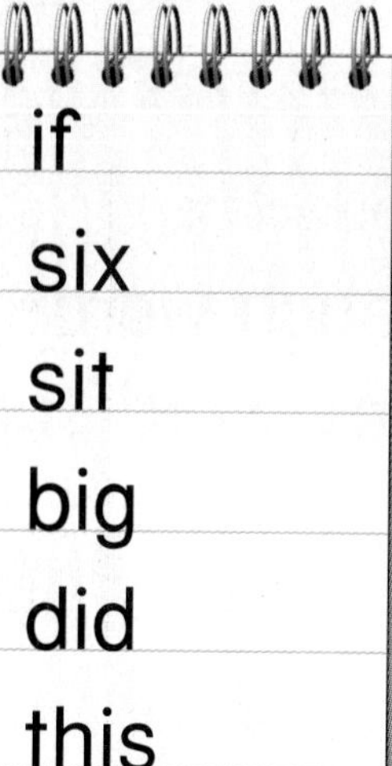

I have ________ little kittens. My kittens will ________ not always be little. Soon they will be ________. The kittens ________ on me. They go to sleep in my lap. They wake up ________ I move. Then ________ is what they do. They cry, "Mew! Mew!" They ________ it just now!

Proofreading

Circle each word that is spelled wrong.
Write the word correctly.

Sis,

You left a bigg mess!

I diid not like it.

Please pick up thes mess now!

Sid

1. ______

2. ______

3. ______

Dictionary Skills

Circle the first letter of each word.
Write each group of words in ABC order.

4. big am can

5. six if has

6. this sit ran

 Name ______

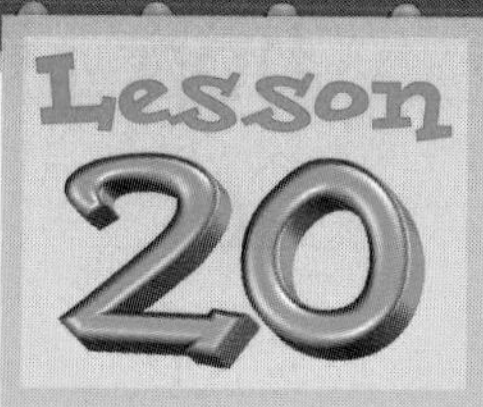

Words with Short o

Say and Write

1. on
2. top
3. not
4. hop
5. hot
6. stop

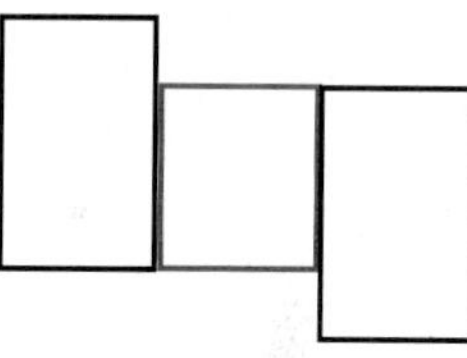

The short o sound can be spelled o.

hop

STOP

stop

on	hop
top	hot
not	stop

Spell and Write

Write the spelling word that completes each sentence.

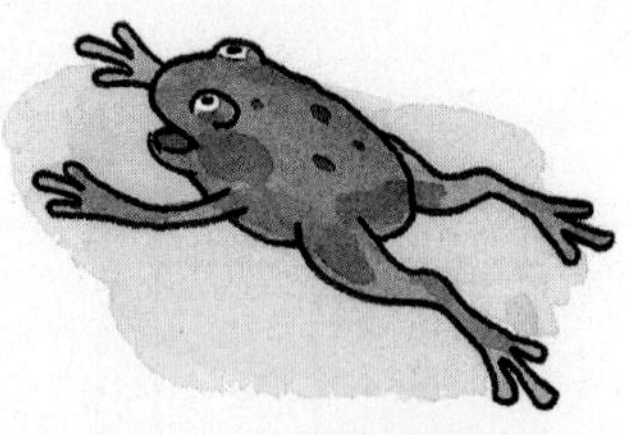

1. A frog can ________.

2. We must ________ and wait.

3. The lamp is ________ the table.

4. Dot is ________.

5. Roxie will ________ come.

6. The little box is on ________.

Name ________

Read and Write

Write the spelling words to complete the story.

on
top
not
hop
hot
stop

Bonnie likes to ________________. She hops and hops. Bonnie hops ________________ the path. She hops on the grass. She does ________________ fall. Then she hops to the ________________ of the hill. When will Bonnie ________________? She will have to stop when she gets too ________________!

Proofreading

Circle each word that is spelled wrong.
Write the word correctly.

Rules for Safe Biking

Put your helmet un.

Do nott ride too fast.

Stap at red lights.

1. ______

2. ______

3. ______

Language Skills

A sentence that asks a question ends with a question mark.

Where is Mopsy?

Write each sentence correctly.

4. Is Mopsy at the top

______

5. Is Mopsy hot

______

6. Will he hop down

______

 Name ______

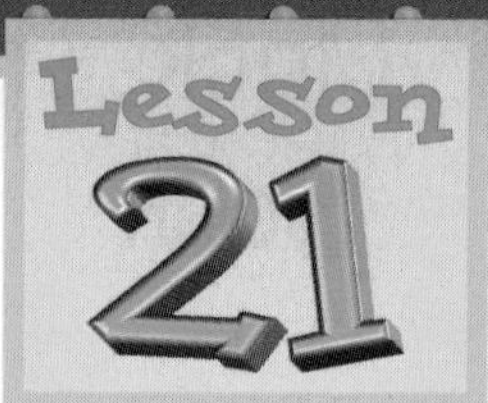

More Words with Short o

Say and Write

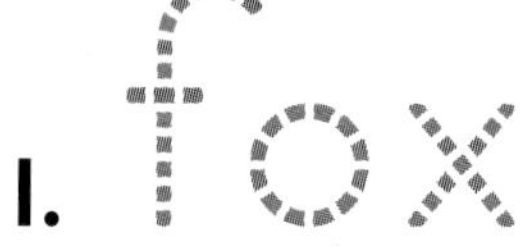

1. fox

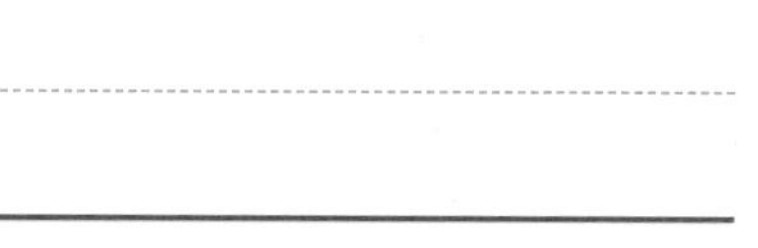

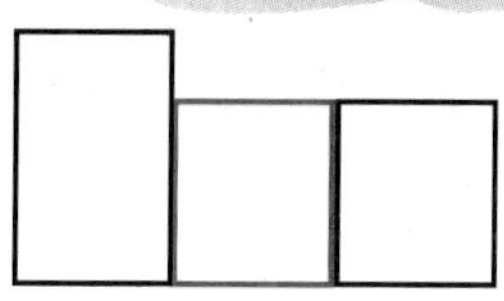

2. mop

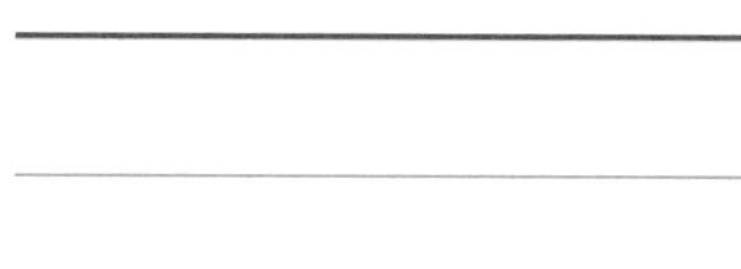

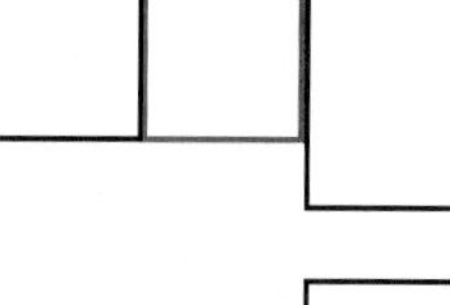

3. job

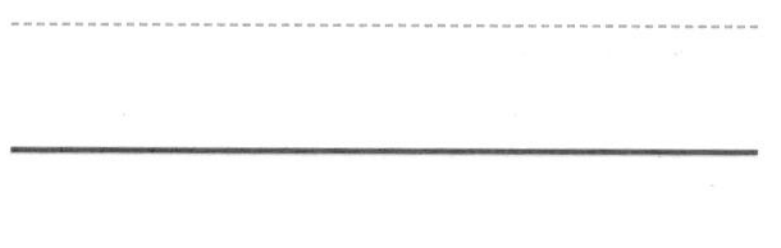

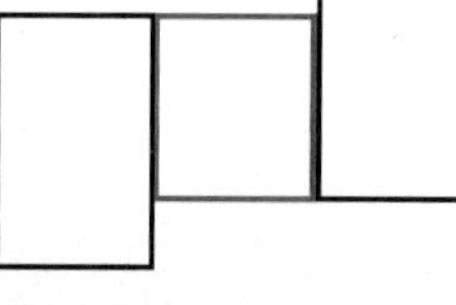

4. box

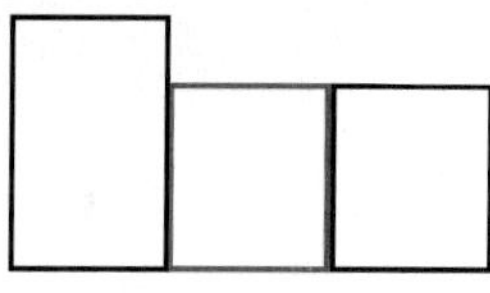

5. lock

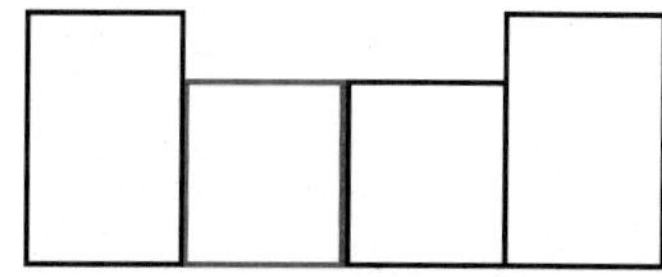

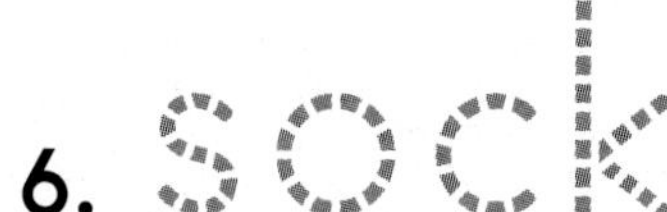

6. sock

The short o sound can be spelled o.

fox

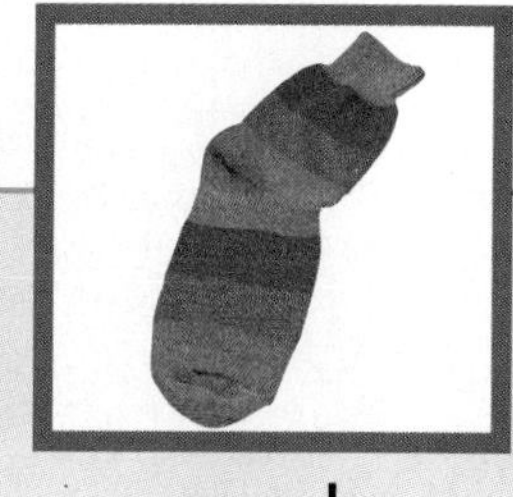

sock

Spell and Write

Write the spelling word that completes each sentence.

fox	lock
mop	sock
job	
box	

1.  Ron lost a ________________.

2.  Dot can ________________ up the mess.

3.  Mom has a ________________ at school.

4.  A ________________ lives in the woods.

5.  Tom put a key in the ________________.

6.  The toys go in a ________________.

Name ________________________________

Read and Write

Write the spelling words to complete the story.

- fox
- mop
- job
- box
- lock
- sock

Bob the ox had a ________________ to do. He had to ________________. A ________________ came in. He had a ________________. The fox took out a brush. "Put this on your ________________," he said.

Bob did it. Then he put a brush on his other sock. He started to mop. "This is fast!" Bob said. "Soon I can ________________ up and go have fun!"

Proofreading

Circle each word that is spelled wrong.
Write the word correctly.

I have a jub to do.

I put the toys in the bax.

Then Mom can moop my room.

1. ______________

2. ______________

3. ______________

Writing

Write a sentence about a job you do.
Use a spelling word.

____

____

 Name ______________________________

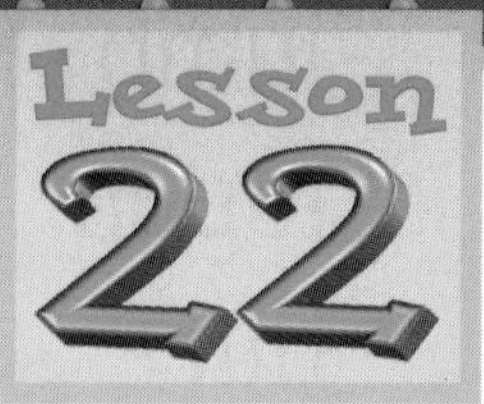

Words with Short u

Say and Write

1. us
2. run
3. fun
4. jump
5. much
6. duck

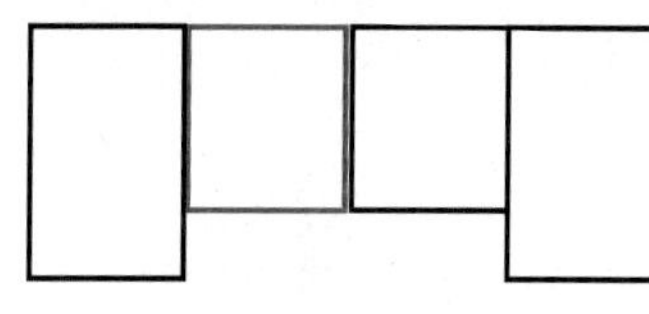

The short u sound can be spelled u.

run

duck

us	jump
run	much
fun	duck

Spell and Write

Write the spelling word that completes each sentence.

1. Bud walks with ____________.

2. They can ____________ fast.

3. Meg and Gus ____________ rope.

4. She feeds the ____________.

5. Josh and Mack had ____________.

6. How ____________ will Gran read?

 Name ____________________

Read and Write

Write the spelling words to complete the selection.

us
run
fun
jump
much
duck

A baby ______________ is called a duckling. A duckling cannot ______________ fast. But it can have ______________. It can ______________ into the water. It can swim, too. The mother duck quacks if a duckling swims too far away. She is saying, "You have gone ______________ too far. Come back to ______________!"

Proofreading

Circle each word that is spelled wrong.
Write the word correctly.

Dusty,

Thanks for coming to see os.

I had fon with you.

I like you very mach.

Sunny

1. ____________

2. ____________

3. ____________

Writing

Write a sentence about someone you like.
Use a spelling word.

 Name ____________

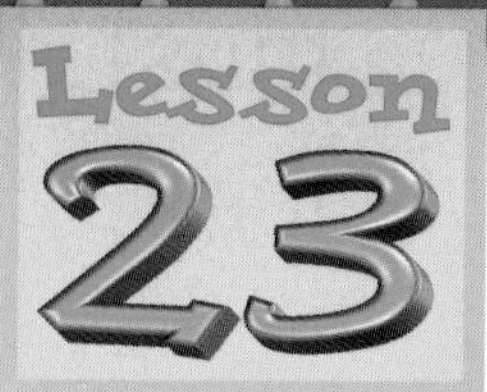

More Words with Short u

Say and Write

1. up
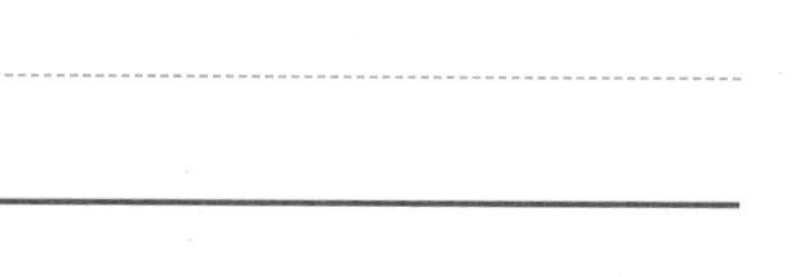

2. cut

3. bus
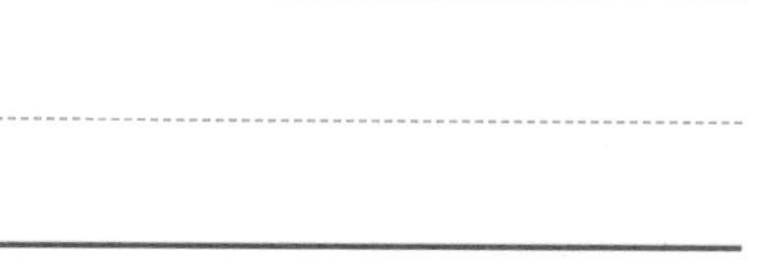

4. but
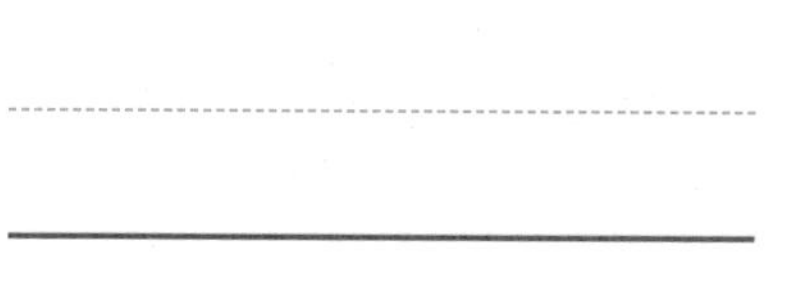

5. must
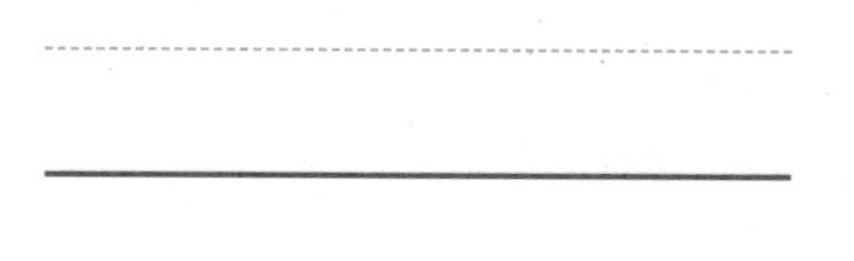

6. just

The short u sound can be spelled u.

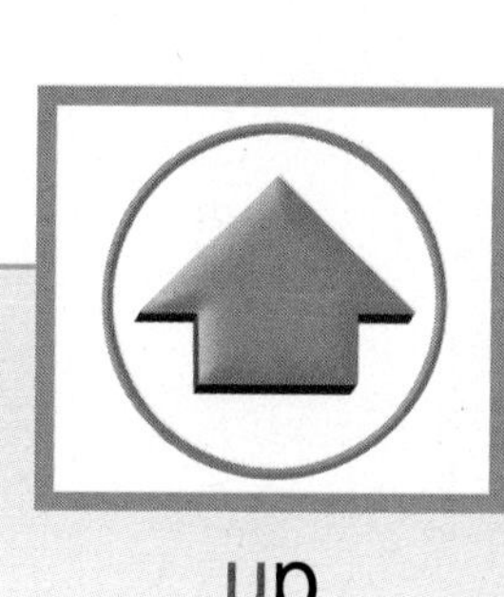
up

bus

up	must
cut	just
bus	
but	

Spell and Write

Write the spelling word that completes each sentence.

1. She will ride the ______________.

2. Russ ______________ pick up the toys.

3. Sunny will ______________ the string.

4. The girls look ______________ alike.

5. It is cold, ______________ there is no snow.

6. The ball goes ______________ and down.

Name ______________________________

Read and Write

Write the spelling words to complete the selection.

up
cut
bus
but
must
just

Do you know what to do on a ________________?

You ________________ sit down when the bus is moving.

You cannot stand ________________. You can play a game.

You can sing a song, too. You can draw, ________________

do not use scissors. You might ________________ yourself.

You can read, or you can ________________ sit and rest.

Proofreading

Circle each word that is spelled wrong.
Write the word correctly.

I jist saw Chuck.

He was on the bos.

We mest get him on our team.

1. ____________

2. ____________

3. ____________

Language Skills

Use is to write about one thing.
Use are to write about more than one thing.

Write the sentences. Use is and are correctly.

4. The cut ____ on my hand.

5. My house ____ up the street.

6. We ____ going home now.

 Name ____________

Unit 4 Review
Lessons 19–23

Missing Letters

Write the missing letter. Then write the word.

big did this

1. d ______ d ______________

2. th ______ s ______________

3. b ______ g ______________

Proofreading

Circle the word that is spelled wrong.
Write it correctly.

on not stop

4. The rain will stap soon. ______________

5. I will play un the sidewalk. ______________

6. I do nat like to stay inside. ______________

Label the Picture

The words in the box go in this picture.
Write each word on the correct line.

job box sock

 Name ____________________

Missing Words

Write the word that completes each sentence.

us fun much

1. We play for ______________ of the day.

2. Would you like to play with ______________?

3. We will have lots of ______________.

Dictionary Skills

Write the words in ABC order.

cut but just

4. ______________

5. ______________

6. ______________

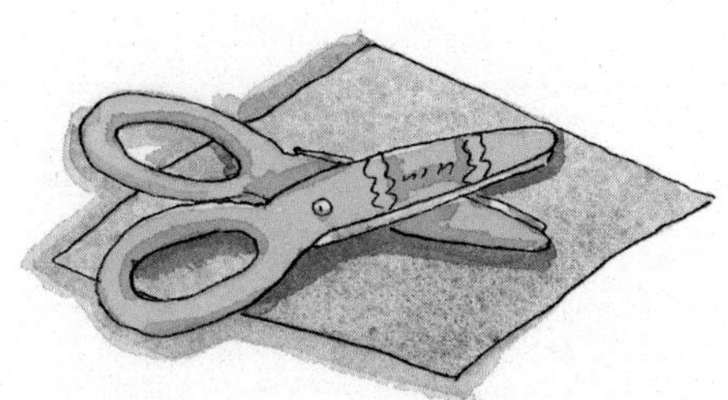

Write About It

Frog is being silly. He puts on silly socks. What do you think will happen next? Write about it. The words in the box may help you.

big	box
did	sock
this	us
on	fun
not	just
stop	but

 Name

Lesson 25 Words with Long a

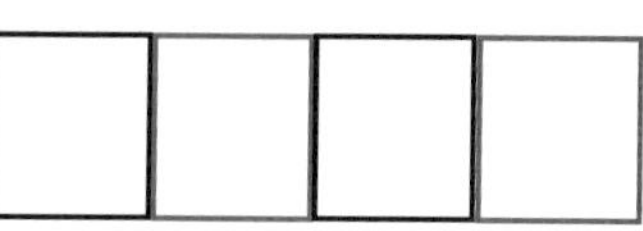

Say and Write

1. name
2. game
3. same
4. made
5. make
6. take

The long a sound can be spelled a_e.

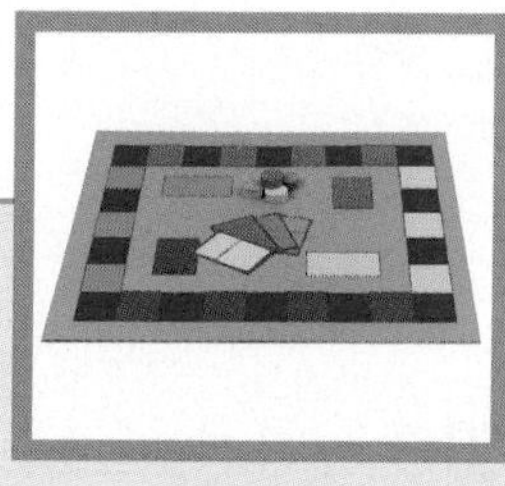
game

take

Spell and Write

Write the spelling word that completes each sentence.

name	made
game	make
same	take

1.  They will ________________ a snack.

2.  Jake and Kate play a ________________.

3. 

The cat's ________________ is Gabe.

4. 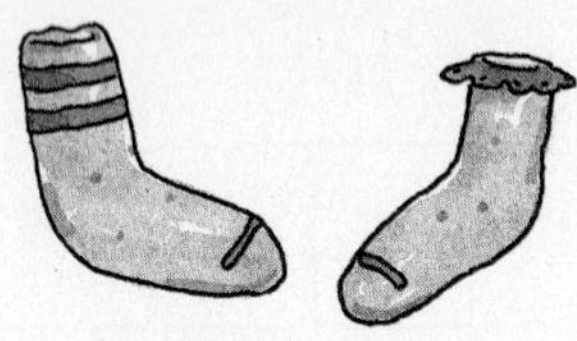 Are the socks the ________________?

5.  Jade will ________________ her lunch.

6.  Tate ________________ a plane.

 Name ________________________________

name
game
same
made
make
take

Read and Write

Write the spelling words to complete the selection.

Polly plays a purple piano.

What is your ________? Play a ________ with your name. To begin, ________ the first letter of your name, such as **P**. Think of words that begin with the ________ letter. Next, ________ a sentence with the words. Then, add more words to the sentence you ________.

Proofreading

Circle each word that is spelled wrong.
Write the word correctly.

Mom let me tak a dog home.

I have to give him a naam.

We will play a geme.

1. ______________________

2. ______________________

3. ______________________

Writing

Write a sentence about a game you like.
Use a spelling word.

____

____

Name ____

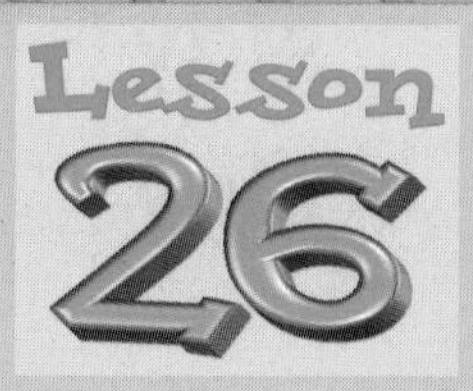

Lesson 26 More Words with Long a

Say and Write

1. day

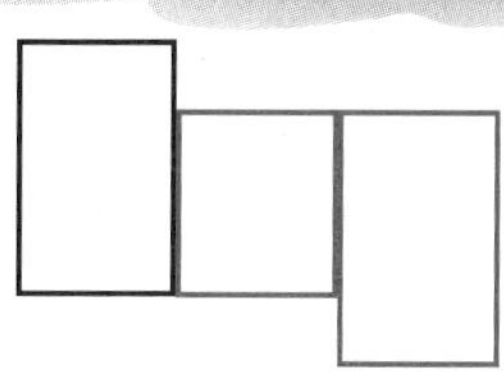

2. may

3. say

4. pay

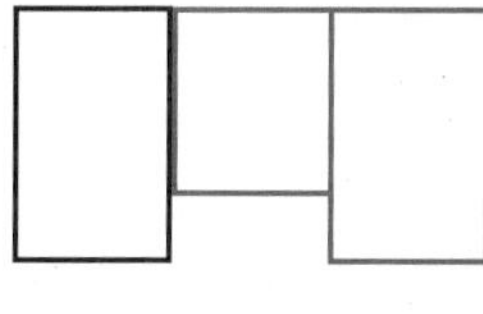

5. stay

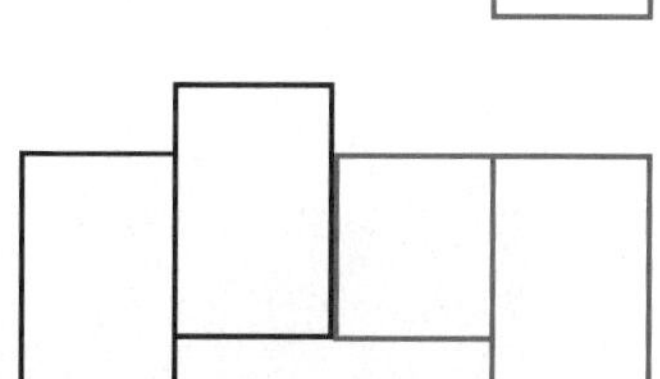

6. play

The long a sound can be spelled ay.

Spell and Write

Write the spelling word that completes each sentence.

day	stay
may	play
say	
pay	

1.  Jay will ______________ for the book.

2.  It is a nice ______________.

3.  Fay must ______________ in bed.

4.  It ______________ rain today.

5.  The kitten likes to ______________.

6.  What will Mom ______________?

Name ______________________________

Read and Write

Write the spelling words to complete the selection.

- day
- may
- say
- pay
- stay
- play

Some work places have a special ________________.

Children ________________ go to work with an adult. They can ________________ all day. They learn about jobs. They have fun, but it is not a time to ________________. The children ________________ they learn a lot. They see how adults work for their ________________.

Proofreading

Circle each word that is spelled wrong. Write the word correctly.

Wayne,

Will you come stae with me?

We could pla a lot.

Please sey you will.

Jake

1. ____

2. ____

3. ____

Language Skills

Sentences begin with a capital letter. Names of people begin with a capital letter, too.

We play with Jay.

Write each sentence correctly.

4. we may play with jay all day.

____

5. he will pay kay today.

____

Name ____

Words with Long e

Say and Write

1. me
2. we
3. he
4. be
5. she
6. eat

The long e sound can be spelled e or ea.

we

eat

me	she
we	eat
he	
be	

Spell and Write

Write the spelling word that completes each sentence.

1.  "Are ________ late?" Lee asked.

2.  It is time to ________.

3.  Is ________ calling Mom?

4.  "Will you help ________?" he asked.

5.  She will ________ awake soon.

6.  Will ________ come and play?

Name ________________

Read and Write

Write the spelling words to complete the story.

- me
- we
- he
- be
- she
- eat

My family sleeps a lot in winter. We need food before ____________ sleep. We ____________ a lot!

Today Mom showed ____________ how to catch fish.

Then ____________ showed my brother. I know ____________ likes fish. Soon we will find a cave.

A cave is a good place to ____________ in winter.

Proofreading

Circle each word that is spelled wrong.
Write the word correctly.

Neal,

Can you bea home by 3:00?

Then wi will go to the game.

Dad said hee will take us.

Jean

1. ____________________

2. ____________________

3. ____________________

Language Skills

Unscramble each sentence and write it.
Use capital letters and periods correctly.

4. my went me with sister

____

5. likes be me she to with

____

6. eat to we pizza went

____

 Name ____________________

More Words with Long e

Say and Write

1. see
2. feet
3. keep
4. tree
5. street
6. three

The long e sound can be spelled ee.

tree

street

see	tree
feet	street
keep	three

Spell and Write

Write the spelling word that completes each sentence.

1. A leaf fell from the ________________.

2. They walk across the ________________.

3. This thing has many ________________.

4. What does she ________________?

5. Pete can ________________ things in the box.

6. The ________________ kittens play all day.

 Name ________________________________

Read and Write

Write the spelling words to complete the story.

- see
- feet
- keep
- tree
- street
- three

Dee's dad took her on a hike with ______________ of her friends. They all live on the same ______________.

"Please ______________ walking on the trail," Dad said.

Something went splash! "What is on the other side of that ______________?" Dad asked.

"I ______________ a creek!" Lee said. "Some kids are in the water. May we get our ______________ wet, too?"

Proofreading

Circle each word that is spelled wrong. Write the word correctly.

We planted a trea.

It will kep growing.

It will be 12 fete tall.

1. ____________

2. ____________

3. ____________

Dictionary Skills

Look up each word in the Spelling Dictionary. Copy the sentence that helps you know what the word means.

4. see

5. street

6. three

Name ____________

Lesson 29 Words with Long i

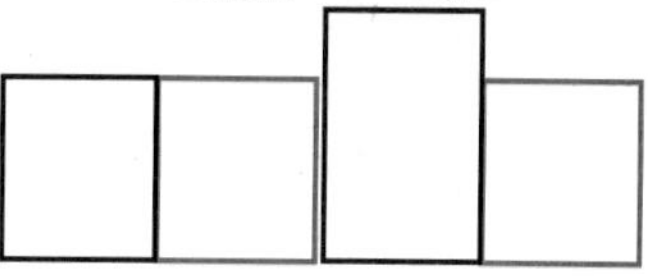

Say and Write

1. ride
2. nine
3. five
4. hide
5. mine
6. time

The long i sound can be spelled i_e.

five

hide

ride	hide
nine	mine
five	time

Spell and Write

Write the spelling word that completes each sentence.

1.  Where did the mouse ______________?

2. I will share ______________ with Mike.

3.  What ______________ is it?

4.  The dog will ______________ in the wagon.

5.  There are ______________ eggs left.

6. 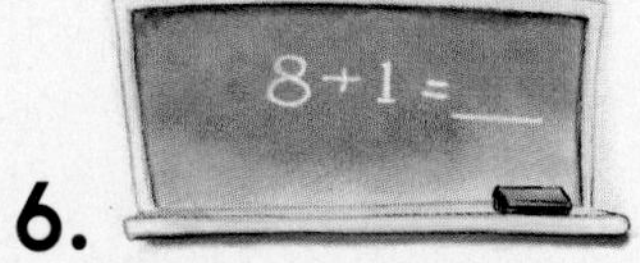

Eight and one make ______________.

 Name ______________________________

Read and Write

Write the spelling words to complete the selection.

ride
nine
five
hide
mine
time

A bike contest can test how well you ______________.

Don't run and ______________. Set up ______________

big cones. Ride around them one at a ______________.

Ride slowly for four or ______________ minutes. Now you

are ready for the contest. You might get to say, "The prize

is ______________!"

Proofreading

Circle each word that is spelled wrong.
Write the word correctly.

I like to ridee my bike.

I'm on it all the tim.

I got it when I was fiv.

1. ____________

2. ____________

3. ____________

Writing

Write two sentences about a bike.
Use two spelling words.

Name ____________

Unit 5 Review

Lessons 25–29

Word Puzzle

Write the spelling word for each clue.

game made take

1. It means "did make."
2. It means "to get."
3. People play this.

Proofreading

Circle the word that is spelled wrong.
Write it correctly.

day say play

4. Clay wants to pla a game. ______
5. What did you sae? ______
6. What a great daay it is! ______

Dictionary Skills

Write the words in ABC order.

we she eat

1. ____________ 2. ____________

3. ____________

Missing Words

Write the word that completes each sentence.

keep three see

4. I went to ____________ a play.

5. One plus two is ____________.

6. May I ____________ this puppy?

 Name ____________

More Missing Words

Write the missing words.

five ride mine

1. ____________________

2. ____________________

3. ____________________

Write About It

Jay and Layla like to play games. What game do you like to play? Write a paragraph about it. Tell how to play the game. The words in the box may help you.

made	eat
game	keep
play	three
day	see
we	mine
she	five

Name ____________________

More Words with Long i

Say and Write

1. my
2. by
3. fly
4. why
5. try
6. cry

The long i sound can be spelled y.

my

fly

Spell and Write

Write the spelling word that completes each sentence.

my	fly
by	why
	try
	cry

1. The baby began to ______________.

2. That little bird wants to ______________!

3. The cat knows ______________ the vase fell.

4. I put on ______________ coat.

5. She will ______________ to skate.

6. The bag is ______________ the door.

Name ______________________________

Read and Write

Write the spelling words to complete the story.

my
by
fly
why
try
cry

I made a kite. I made ____________ kite from a bag. I wanted it to ____________ up high. People stood ____________ me. They asked ____________ I used a bag. I wanted to ____________ it. That's why.

The bag did not fly very high, but I did not ____________.

I just made another kite.

Proofreading

Circle each word that is spelled wrong.
Write the word correctly.

This is miy bird.

He likes to flye.

He likes to sit bi me.

1. ______

2. ______

3. ______

Writing

Write two sentences about a bird.
Use two spelling words.

Name ______

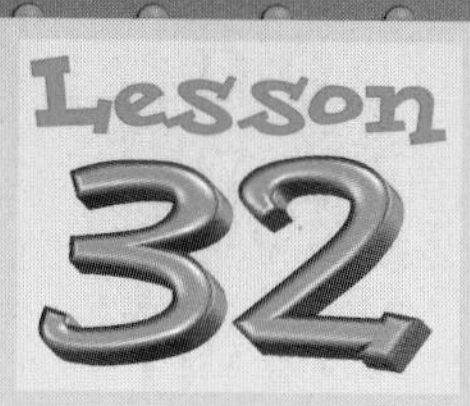

Lesson 32 Words with Long o

Say and Write

1. so
2. go
3. old
4. told
5. cold
6. over

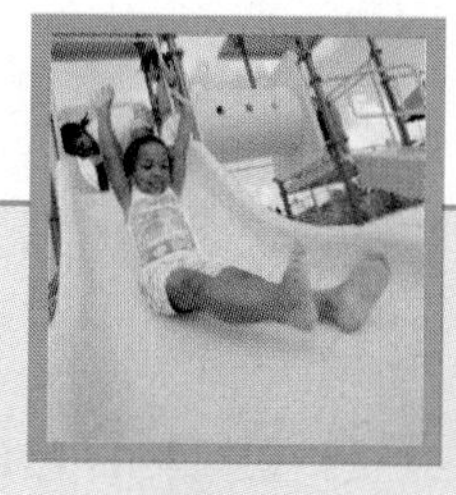
go

cold

The long o sound can be spelled o.

so | old
go | told
cold
over

Spell and Write

Write the spelling word that completes each sentence.

1. The shop was closed, ________________ we left.

2. Jo ________________ Bo a joke.

3. Mom held the paper ________________ her head.

4. The ball will ________________ far.

5. The little dog was ________________.

6. The big tree was very ________________.

 Name ________________________________

Read and Write

Write the spelling words to complete the story.

- so
- go
- old
- told
- cold
- over

JoJo wanted to ______________ to a special place. She wanted to go ______________ the rainbow. JoJo packed an ______________ bag. She got her coat in case it was ______________. JoJo ______________ Gran about her plan. Gran wanted to go, too, ______________ they went together. Good luck, JoJo and Gran!

Proofreading

Circle each word that is spelled wrong.
Write the word correctly.

Mom,

May I ask Lin to come ovr?

She is soo much fun.

Then can we goe for pizza?

Joey

1. ______

2. ______

3. ______

Language Skills

Use was to write about one thing.
Use were to write about more than one thing.

Write the sentences. Use was and were correctly.

4. We ____ in an old store.

5. Mom ____ by the milk.

6. I told Mom I ____ cold.

 Name ______

More Words with Long o

Say and Write

1. home

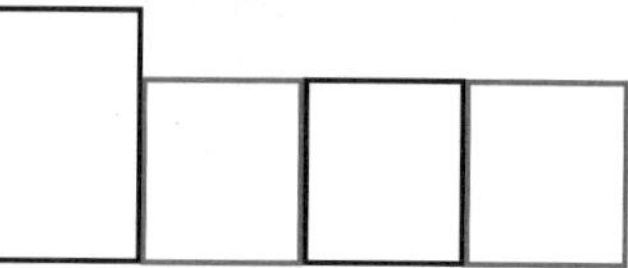

2. hope

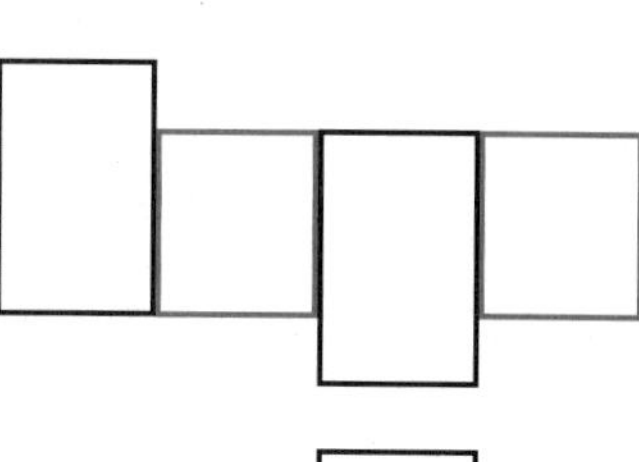

3. note

4. nose

5. road

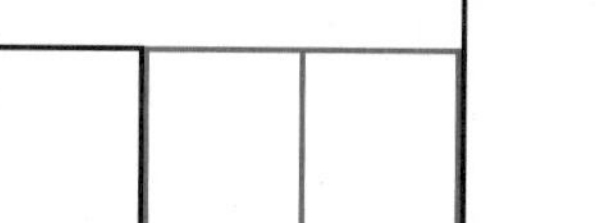

6. coat

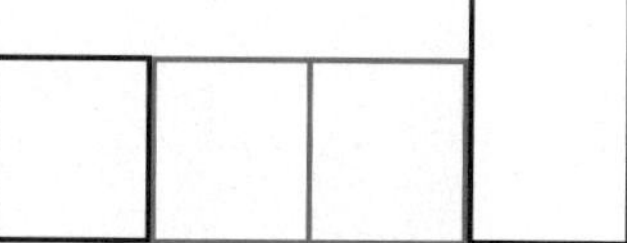

The long o sound can be spelled o_e or oa.

home

road

Spell and Write

Write the spelling word that completes each sentence.

home	road
hope	coat
note	
nose	

1.  I ride down the ______________.

2.  We ______________ it rains today.

3.  My ______________ is green.

4.  He has a big red ______________.

5.  Mr. Lo's ______________ is in a big city.

6. 

Joan wrote me a ______________.

 Name ______________________________

Read and Write

Write the spelling words to complete the story.

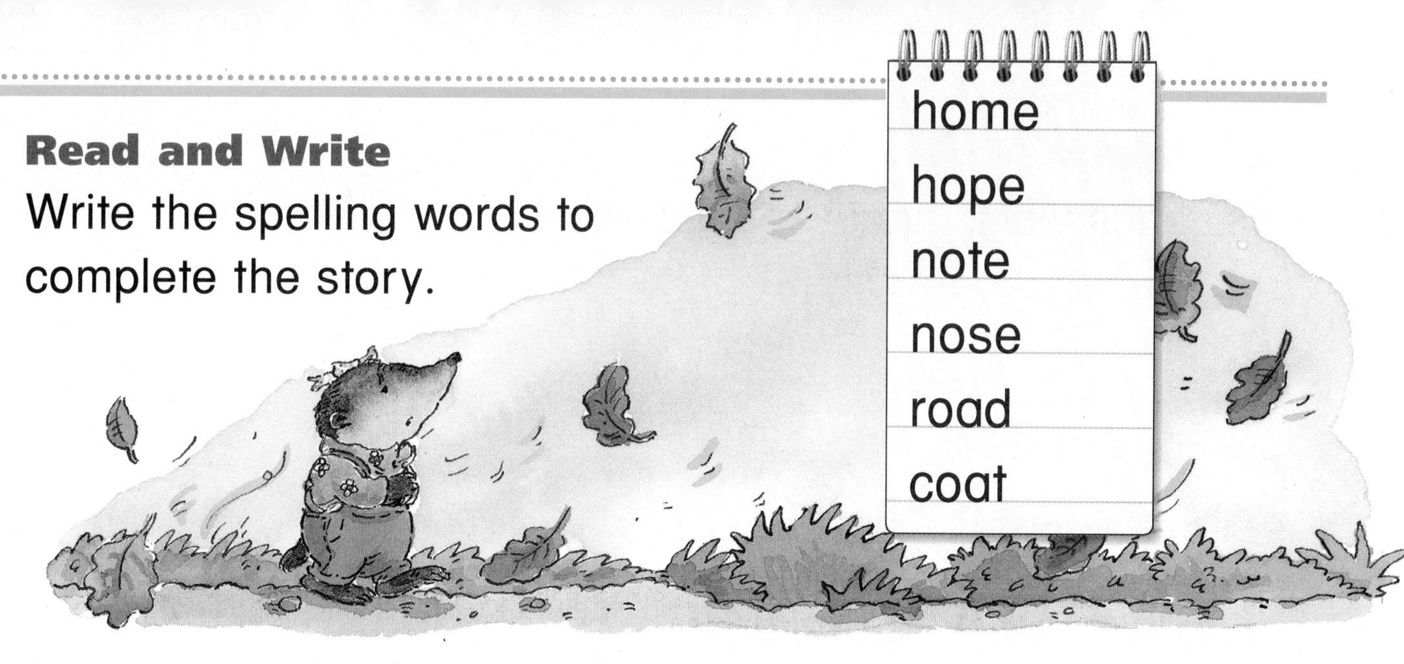

One day Mole wanted to take a walk. Dad was not at

________________. Mole wrote Dad a ________________.

Then she walked down the ________________. She walked

a long way. A cold wind came. Mole's ________________

was blue. She wanted her warm ________________.

"I ________________ I am not lost!" she said. Then Mole

saw her house. She smiled and went inside.

Proofreading

Circle each word that is spelled wrong. Write the word correctly.

Mom,

I lost my cote.

I hoap you are not mad.

I will stay hoam to look for it.

Joan

1. ______

2. ______

3. ______

Dictionary Skills

Circle the first letter of each word. Then write the words in ABC order.

4. road home note

______

______

______

5. told nose go

______

______

______

Words with the Vowel Sound in food

Say and Write

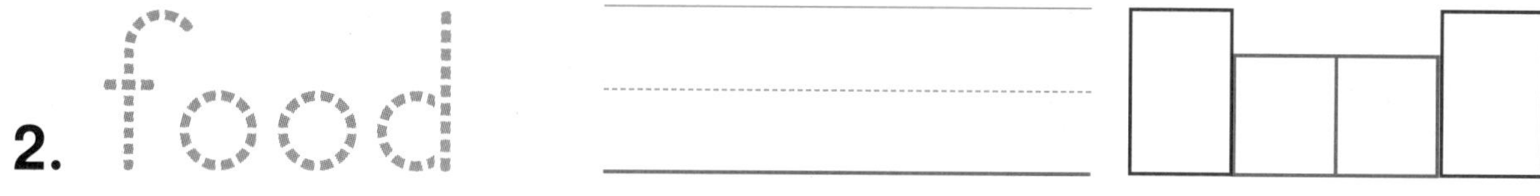

1. zoo
2. food
3. room
4. moon
5. soon
6. school

The vowel sound in food can be spelled oo.

zoo

school

zoo	moon
food	soon
room	school

Spell and Write

Write the spelling word that completes each sentence.

1.  What jumped over the ______________?

2.  Where do you go to ______________?

3.  Will cleaned his ______________.

4.  It will be dark ______________.

5.  We had fun at the ______________.

6. 

Dad and Joel shop for ______________.

 Name ______________________________

Read and Write

Write the spelling words to complete the selection.

zoo
food
room
moon
soon
school

Would you like to camp at a ________________? At one zoo, you can sleep in a ________________ with beds. You can sleep under the ________________ and stars, too. You can give ________________ to the animals. Your class from ________________ might want to go zoo camping. Find out about zoo camping ________________!

Proofreading

Circle each word that is spelled wrong.
Write the word correctly.

I went on a schul trip.

We went to the zo.

We gave foode to the seals.

1. ____________

2. ____________

3. ____________

Writing

Write two sentences about a zoo.
Use two spelling words.

Lesson 35

More Words with the Vowel Sound in food

Say and Write

1. too 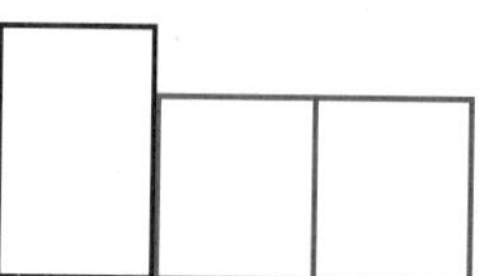

2. who 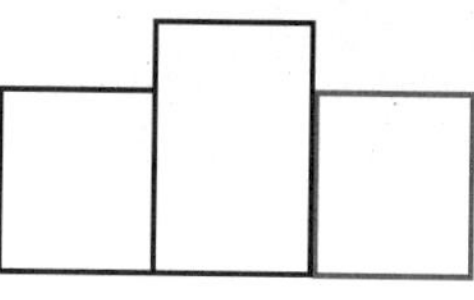

3. two  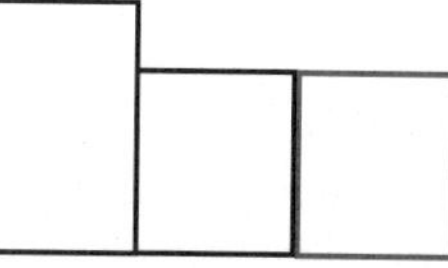

4. do 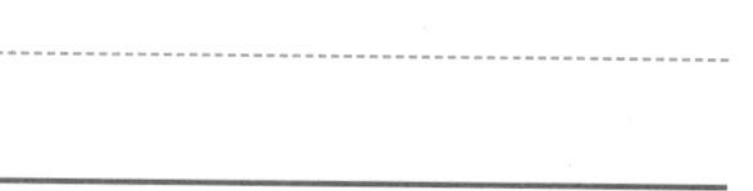 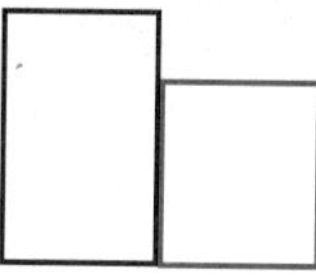

5. shoe 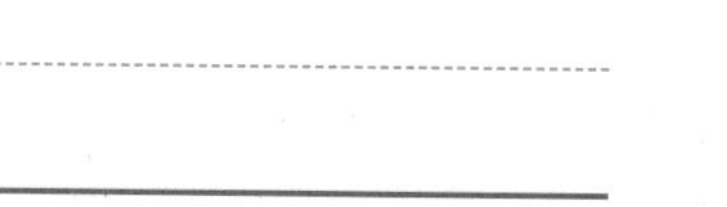 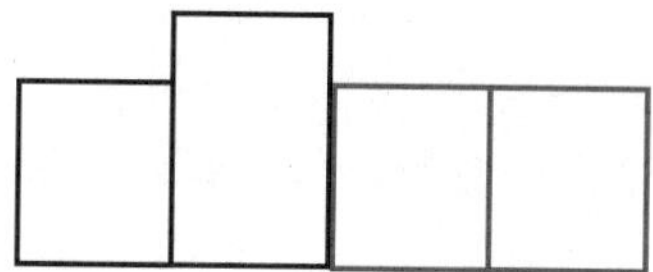

6. you 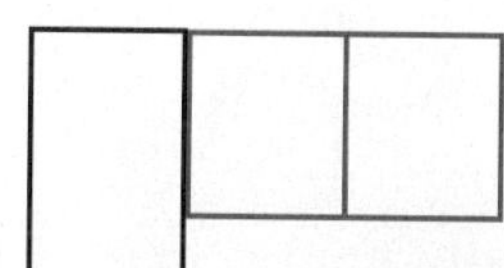

The vowel sound in food can be spelled oo, o, oe, or ou.

two

too

shoe

you

Spell and Write

Write the spelling word that completes each sentence.

too	shoe
who	you
two	
do	

1. It's time to ______________ our work.

2. The hat is ______________ big.

3. Stu, where are ______________?

4. Lou said, "I know ______________ you are."

5. The bike has ______________ wheels now.

6. Boo has my ______________.

 Name ______________________________

Read and Write

Write the spelling words to complete the selection.

too
who
two
do
shoe
you

Look at your ________ feet. Is there a ________ on each foot? Shoes keep your feet safe. Shoes should not be ________ big or too small.

No one knows ________ made the first shoes. Early people made them from animal skins. Now ________ can buy shoes in a store. What kind of shoes ________ you like to wear?

Proofreading

Circle each word that is spelled wrong.

Write the word correctly.

Sue,

How much doo you like the circus?

I have tou tickets.

Will yoe come with me?

Dooley

1. ______

2. ______

3. ______

Language Skills

Use to to mean into. Use too to mean more than enough.

Use two to mean the number after one.

Write the sentences. Use to, two, and too correctly.

4. Who are those ____ girls?

5. That shoe is ____ big.

6. Did they go ____ the store?

Name ______

Lesson 36

Unit 6 Review

Lessons 31–35

Missing Letter

Write y in each box. Then write the word.

my why try

1. tr ☐ = ____________ 2. wh ☐ = ____________

3. m ☐ = ____________

Proofreading

Circle the word that is spelled wrong. Write it correctly.

go told over

4. I can fly ovr a house. ____________

5. I can goa to the top of a tree. ____________

6. I toald my dad to look at me. ____________

Rhyming Words

Help Toad find her way home. For each word on the trail, write the rhyming word from the box.

hope	road	coat

1. ________________ 2. ________________

3. ________________

 Name ________________________

Missing Words

Write the word that completes each sentence.

room soon school

1. We must go home ______.

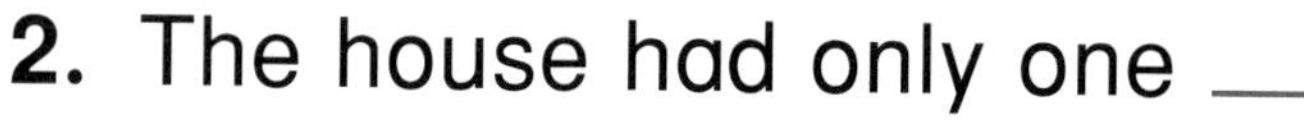

2. The house had only one ______.

3. It is time to go to ______.

Dictionary Skills

Write the words in ABC order.

who shoe you

4. ______

5. ______

6. ______

Write About It

Mole will go fishing tomorrow. What will you do tomorrow? Write a paragraph about it. The words in the box may help you.

why	home
my	room
told	road
go	over
who	shoe
you	school

 Name

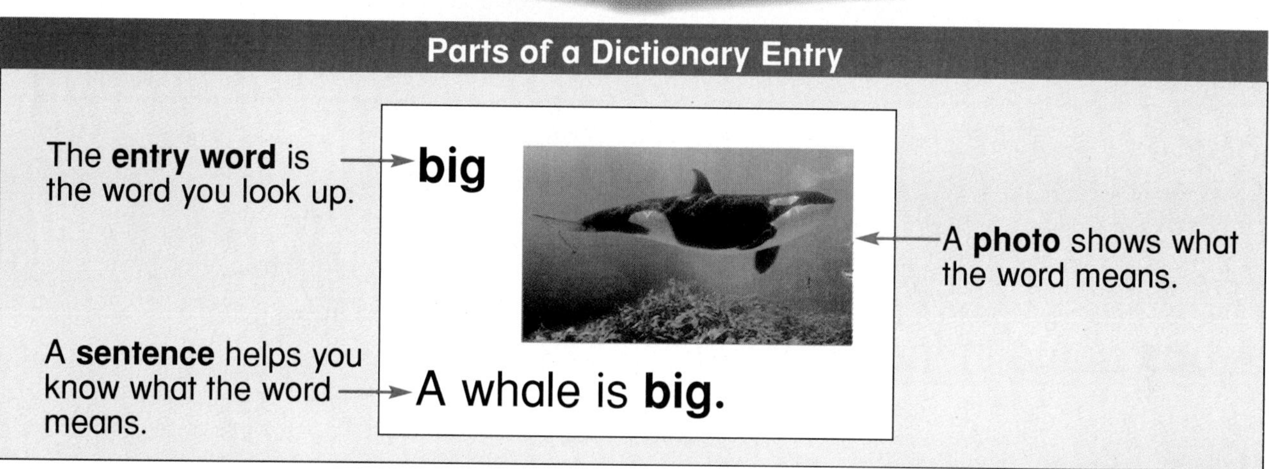

am

I **am** happy.

at

He is **at** work.

be

We will **be** home soon.

best

She is the **best** artist.

big

A whale is **big.**

box

A **box** came in the mail.

bus

We ride a **bus** to school.

but

I am short, **but** my brother is tall.

by

I sat **by** my mom.

Cc

can

I **can** ride a bike.

coat

My **coat** keeps me warm.

cold

A snowy day is **cold.**

cry

The baby began to **cry.**

cut

I **cut** the paper.

day

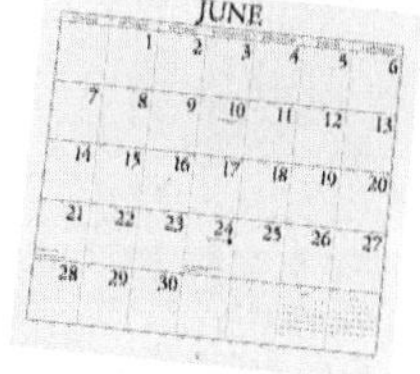

A calendar shows each **day** in a month.

did

Look what I **did**!

do

I **do** my work.

duck

A **duck** can swim.

eat

I like to **eat** peanut butter.

end

He is at the **end** of the line.

fast

A horse can run **fast.**

feet

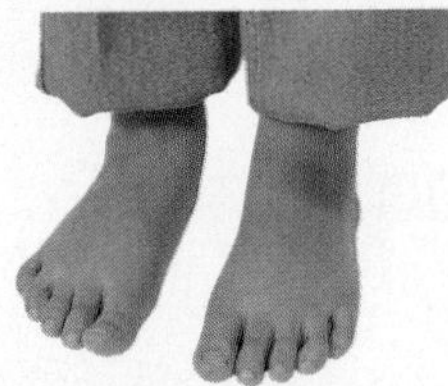

I have two **feet.**

five

I can count to **five.**

fly

Birds use their wings to **fly.**

food

Which **food** do you like?

fox

A **fox** has a bushy tail.

fun

She is having **fun.**

Gg

game

Do you want to play a **game**?

get

My mom will **get** a present.

go

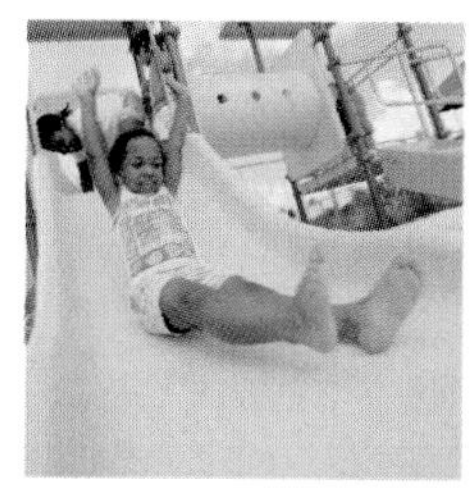

I **go** down the slide.

Hh

hand

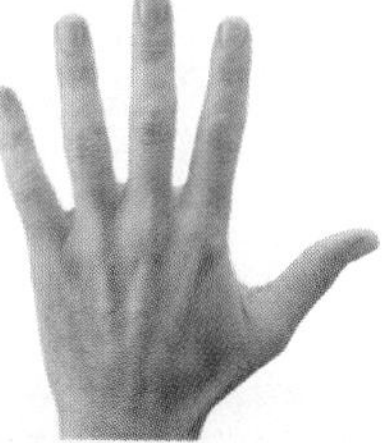

A **hand** has five fingers.

has

She **has** a new pet.

have

I **have** a pumpkin.

he

He likes to read.

help

Dad will **help** me ride my bike.

hide

I can **hide** behind a tree.

home 

That is their **home.**

hop 

I can **hop.**

hope 

I **hope** she picks me.

hot 

The food is **hot.**

if 

I can do it **if** I try.

in 

The fish is **in** the bowl.

is 

That man **is** her grandfather.

it

This is my chair. **It** is very big.

job

Her **job** is to help animals.

jump

I can **jump** high.

just

She looks **just** like me.

keep

She will **keep** the puppy.

last

She is the **last** one in line.

lock

I have a **lock** for my bike.

made

We **made** cookies.

make

I can **make** breakfast.

may

It **may** rain today.

me

Mom reads to **me.**

mine

The ball is **mine.**

moon

The **moon** shines at night.

mop

Use a **mop** to clean the floor.

much

Much of the grass is brown.

must

I **must** rake the leaves.

my

Do you like **my** cap?

Nn

name

I can write my **name.**

nine

Eight plus one is **nine.**

nose

My puppy licks my **nose.**

not

She is **not** happy.

note

I wrote Mom a **note.**

Oo

old

Their truck is **old.**

on

The frog is **on** the plant.

over

The bridge goes **over** the water.

pay

She will **pay** the man.

pet

My **pet** is a cat.

play

I **play** baseball.

quit

Please **quit** making that noise!

ran

We **ran** in a race.

red

I like the color **red.**

ride

Some people **ride** camels.

road

Where does that **road** go?

room

She is in her **room.**

run

They can **run** fast.

Ss

same

We have the **same** kind of shirt.

sat

He **sat** on the steps.

say

I **say** hello.

school

It's time for **school.**

see

I can **see** the stars.

seven

Six and one make **seven.**

she

She can cook.

shoe

Is this your **shoe**?

sick

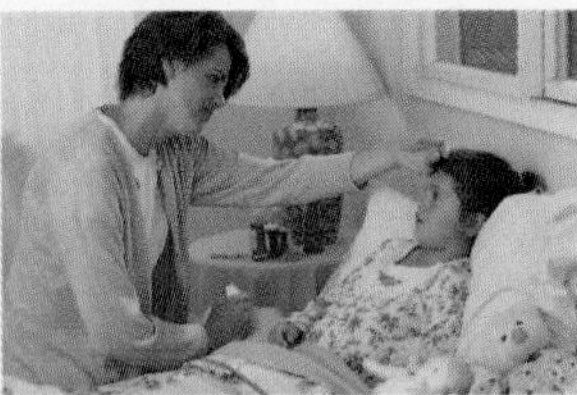

She is **sick.**

sit

They **sit** at a table to do their work.

six

6

Five and one make **six.**

so

He was tired, **so** he went to sleep.

sock

My **sock** has stripes.

soon

We will go home **soon.**

stay

We will **stay** here all day.

stop

The sign tells us to **stop.**

street

We live on this **street.**

take

I will **take** a cookie.

tell

I **tell** her my name.

ten

10

I can count to **ten.**

that

That is the answer.

this

I made **this** by myself.

three

3

Two plus one is **three.**

time

What **time** is it?

told

She **told** me a funny story.

too

His hat is **too** big.

top

She is at the **top.**

tree

A **tree** is a tall plant.

try

He will **try** to hit the ball.

two

One plus one is **two.**

Uu

up

The balloons are going **up.**

us

She teaches **us.**

van

They have a red **van.**

we

We are friends.

went

Some ducks **went** into the water.

wet

We get **wet** in the rain.

when

Flowers bloom **when** it is spring.

who

Who is at the door?

why

He asks **why** the bus is late.

with

The sandwich comes **with** a pickle.

you

Do **you** like ice cream?

zoo

This animal lives in a **zoo.**

Commonly Misspelled Words

about	girl	one	too
am	have	or	two
and	her	our	very
are	him	outside	want
because	his	people	was
came	house	play	went
can	in	said	were
color	into	school	when
every	know	some	with
family	like	teacher	would
friend	little	their	your
friends	me	there	
get	my	they	